4C – Building and Developing a Ministry Team in Your Church

Scott Douglas

4C – Building and Developing a Ministry Team in Your Church

ISBN 9781708069704

Printed in the United States of America

Few things are more important in leading a healthy organization than developing the right culture. It has been said that "culture eats strategy for breakfast." Without the right culture, it is difficult to accomplish your mission. This is why developing an effective ministry team is vital to the church accomplishing its mission. Scott Douglas has written an excellent book on the best practices for developing high-capacity ministry teams. Whether you are a seasoned leader, or just getting started on the journey, you will find this work helpful.

Chad Keck, Ph.D.
Senior Pastor, FBC Kettering OH

Scott Douglas has effectively written a workbook to teach church leaders how to team up in accomplishing a ministry vision. Church ministries too often become silos as Douglas pinpoints. This book does not just identify problems among church leaders and ministries, but offers real life solutions. I recommend this text as a resource for the classroom because it provides a rationale for a biblical model of teams. I recommend it to church leaders because it gets right to the point of employing a team model in accomplishing the Great Commission.

Larry Purcell, Ph.D.
Kentucky Baptist Convention

Someone has said, "Teamwork makes the dream work". Most things we do in ministry are done better when they are done with a committed team pulling together in the same direction. Most pastors and church leaders, however, do not feel equipped with the necessary skills to assemble a great team. Scott's book will provide helpful tips along with proven practices toward that end. I recommend it to you.

Dr. Todd Gray
Executive Director-Treasurer for Kentucky Baptist Convention

Dedication Page

No book is ever written in a vacuum, especially one as dynamic and personal as this one is. As I've read through what I've written before and revised for this version, I was able to think about the people I've worked alongside over the last decade plus of ministry. I'm so grateful for the chance to have some real friends in those rooms, especially when there were hard days.

To our team at Emmanuel, thank you for leading alongside me. We have a lot of fun, and I love getting the texts and DMs from you guys where we can laugh a little about the stresses of ministry. I love that we take our work seriously and we're all-in for the health, strength, and direction of the church. I also love that we don't take ourselves too seriously so we can have a lot of laughs in our meetings. You all truly are a joy to serve alongside.

A book like this is written largely with the input, from afar, of writers and leaders who have been influential in what they've left behind in books, articles, and blogs. I'm indebted to all I've learned from you. Thank you for your transparency and vulnerability to share not only the success in leadership but also the flops. You are more than footnotes in this book. You have all had a profound impact in my life and ministry.

Finally, this book is specifically dedicated to my oldest, Samuel. I will never forget sitting in the doctor's office with Mommy when we found out we were going to be parents. I loved you all the way to Louisville and Pluto and back from that very first day. You continue to bring so much joy to our home, and my heart loved nothing more than hearing you confess Jesus and being able to baptize you. I love that we ride bikes, play catch, watch the "Go Cards" on TV, that you geek out on History and NatGeo like I do, that you like playing chess, and that you'll just look around with eyes of wonder. I love you buddy.

Contents

Foreword

Love them or hate them, the New York Yankees put together what is arguably the greatest baseball team of all time in 1998. Stars dotted the landscape in every direction—on the mound, in the field, at the plate, on the bench, and in the manager's office. Winning the American League East Division by 22 games, they then dismantled their postseason opponents en route to a World Series sweep of the San Diego Padres. This second of four championships in five years was most impressive—a team with such talent, playing in New York's pressure-cooker media market, could have easily imploded because of ego and envy. But this was a true dream team, one on which each player performed his role with excellence, humility, and a desire to be a part of something truly great. And we're still talking about it decades later.

Imagine for a second being a part of a team like that. Far too often, the story is the opposite—splintered staff relationships, stagnant churches, frustrated pastors, and disillusioned church members. But what if it doesn't have to be that way? What if a Dream Team of competent and cohesive staff members, men and women who live with godly character, served at your church? Yes, the one you currently serve.
As Scott Douglas shows, not only is a Dream Team possible, it is entirely probable if you apply the principles you'll find from his study and experience.

Being a part of a team isn't easy. Sometimes I wish I had played and coached golf or tennis, an individual sport done in isolation, where the actions and failures of others have little to no effect on the outcome of the match. But I've always played and coached team sports. There's something beautiful about teams. Scary, yes, but beautiful. A group of individuals with personal ambitions and motives comes together for a common cause, humbly sacrificing personal gain for the good of the whole--that's beautiful. We are impressed by individual accomplishment, but we are inspired by team accomplishment. it's rare and powerful.

Having coached at every level of amateur baseball, and having served at every level of ministry in the church, I've seen teams of all kinds. I've played on and coached for teams that won, teams that lost, teams that overachieved, teams that underachieved. Scott provides the game plan necessary to achieve what God desires our churches to have: Leadership Dream Teams filled with individuals who love Jesus, love each other, and love the people they serve.

In each chapter, Scotts shows us how through illustrations sure to delight sports fans. He tells us how through instruction sure to inform both the novice and the experienced minister. And he challenges us to get to work through clear steps sure to guide church staffs of any size.

You don't have to live and minister in a Big League town to have a great team. It's not about market size. It's about determining here and now to build and maintain the type of ministry Dream Team God wants for you. Jesus did it and his Holy Spirit can empower you to do the same. Digest the instruction, learn from the illustrations, and follow the steps Scott lays out in Dream Teams. When you do, my prayer is that you'll still be talking about that team decades later.

It's possible. Press on.

Dr. Brad J. Burns
Founder, Baseball Pastor Ministries

Preface

A second version of a book is a rare luxury in publishing. In a lot of ways, it lets you go back and fix some things you wish you could have in the original. When I completed the draft for *Dream Teams*, I was so excited to have finished a book and get it published. So much of it came from being in a second chair role in a church and writing out my thoughts and perspectives of what I wished could be on our ministry staff.

But that first version was written as a second chair and was written more for churches that had a permanent, full-time, regularly-in-the-office staff. After *Dream Teams* was released, I got some good feedback from a friend that basically said he liked what I had to say but he felt like it could only be used by larger churches. And since I became a lead pastor, I've learned the perspective of leadership changes dramatically just by moving over a chair on the bench.

That's why this version is a little different. It's written with a little bit of experience in the lead role. It's also written to really try to engage churches of all sizes. That's why I'll talk about how important digital communication is to develop a team concept. I'll even try to explain how group texts can be used to help foster a ministry team. Lastly, the chapter on character will be emphasized even more after the outbreak of news impacting churches and ministry leaders. When our position and influence outpaces our character, we're doomed.

If you read *Dream Teams*, you'll find a lot of the concepts the same. That's intentional. I really think the 4C model had value, and could be really useful for churches to implement. Where *Dream Teams* failed, I hope *4C* is better suited to help you and your church be stronger, more faithful, and more effective together.

Introduction
Dreaming of a Ministry Team

When I was 10 years old, I watched the Dream Team take over the 1992 Olympics in absolutely dominating fashion. For two weeks, the best players in the world took on overmatched and at times star-struck competition. It wasn't just an all-star team, it was filled with household names: Jordan, Bird, Magic, Stockton, Barkley, and Malone. They never called a time out, never trailed in a game, often signed autographs on the court, and won by an average of 44 points per game.

What separated that team from subsequent teams that struggled (the 2002 Olympic bronze medalists, the 2006 World Cup 6th place, and the 2019 World Cup 7th place) wasn't talent, it was chemistry. Every Team USA fielded since 1992 has featured professional players from the highest levels of basketball. Most have been on all-star teams. Many have won championships. But it didn't always translate to success in the international circuit. The struggling teams averaged fewer assists, often had more conflict on the roster, and weren't captained by leaders in the locker room.

Maybe your church feels that way too. You feel like you're part of a really talented ministry staff, but something just doesn't feel right. When you look around you see really competent, qualified, and effective leaders. But when you come together something doesn't gel. You don't find yourselves working together, you don't have good communication, you don't have any real rapport or friendship with others, or you just don't feel like you're heading the same direction.

Ministry in those kinds of dynamics isn't much fun, is it? I've been there. I'm sure you have too. Maybe you're in it now. It's frustrating feeling like everyone in leadership in the church is operating on their own without any real cohesion, and you dread the next staff meeting because you know you'd rather be in the dentist chair. At least there something gets done, unlike your meetings. You know the church could do so much more for the Kingdom, if it could just feel like a team.

That's where I want this book to be a help to you and your church. I believe a team is possible in your church's leadership. You don't have to be a multi-staff church with a big full-time staff to have a team environment. This is something that can happen in any size church with any dynamic of staffing or volunteers. Our team largely works remote because we're a smaller church. But we maintain a team environment through digital communication and committing to healthy meetings. That's where the singular idea of a team comes into play: that a team is made of people who have been called by God, who have character necessary for leadership, are gifted and skilled for leadership, and help create chemistry.

Through this book you'll hear it called 4C. Calling. Character. Competency. Chemistry. Four areas of emphasis that can change the way your church ministers by looking at the staff or leadership and creating a truly healthy, cooperative, and unified team concept. A team is where individual leaders come together with their personality, gifts, skills, calling, and abilities and are able to multiply their impact by working towards a common goal. For churches, it's fulfilling the Great Commission by seeing people live out the Great Commandment.

If you're a rookie ministry leader or a seasoned veteran, there is so much you can take from this book. In the first chapter, we'll lay out the blueprint for a ministry team by identifying what is, and isn't, a team. Then we'll work through each of the four C's. We'll end by looking at what it means to hire for a ministry team and how to execute the game plan for developing a true ministry team. You can't just snap your finger and become a team overnight. It will take time, and you'll likely experience significant growing pains in developing a team mindset. That's why at the end of every chapter there will be reflection questions for you to think about. And on my website, scottmdouglas.com, you'll be able to find a series of worksheets you can work through with your ministry staff.

Chapter 1
The Blueprint for a Ministry Team

"I'm not looking for the best players, I'm looking for the right ones." This line from the 2004 movie *Miracle* about the 1980 US Olympic hockey team stands out because it shows the focus of coach Herb Brooks: to develop a team. This was necessary because, after completing an endless series of drills he has the plays announce their name and who they play for. Early in the movie they say their name and their college team, but after a late-night conditioning drill, the captain says "I play for the United States of America." At that moment, Brooks knew they got it. They were a team. And that team would pull off one of the biggest upsets in history, knocking off the Soviets on their way to a gold medal.

It's possible to have that same kind of team and attitude on a ministry staff. Lead pastors are like the coach who molds and shapes the culture, sets goals, and promotes a vision for what can happen if there is a team. Others on the leadership can be like team captains, the influencers and catalysts within the staff to support and build on the vision cast by the lead pastor. Finally, it's up to every member of the leadership to recognize their role on the team and buy into the unifying goal and purpose of the leadership.

Everything in this book is built on this one statement: It is possible to build and develop an effective ministry team. I know, that's too simple. But it's true, and it's intentionally written that simple. Too often I think we don't build a team because we think it will be too much work or too hard. But it's possible to have a leadership team, because no matter the size of a church or the experience of the leaders, a team is attainable by focusing on the 4 C's.

Let that sink in for a minute. That meeting you're dreading? It could be a helpful and encouraging time of decision-making and action. That ministry event you feel alone planning? It could be something others buy into as well. The ding on your cell phone you're trying to ignore? It could be an opportunity for relationship development.

What Teams Don't Look Like

If we examine many churches around us, it's safe to say the idea of ministry *teams* isn't being realized. Many churches operate like a golf team. On a golf team, everyone plays their round and then the scores are totaled up and the team with the lowest score wins. Is that really a team? I don't think so. I'd argue it's more a compilation, rather than a collaborative, effort.

Churches operate the same way when the staff ministers operate in their roles independent of each other. They might come together for occasional meetings, but are not invested in others' ministries, and do not share goals that can only be achieved by collaborative effort. They may wear the same jersey, but they aren't a true team. The list of achievements are compiled on a white board or a summary report, and the church can be viewed as a success because the individual ministries are doing great. But individual results aren't always reflective of a team effort or team mindset. Here are some ways we see a lot of churches operate with this approach:

- *Silo Approach* – In this approach, the individual ministries operate next to each other, but their work, results, ambitions, goals, and values aren't connected to one another or to the overall vision and direction of the church. There's little coordination between ministry leaders, little synthesis of core values and direction, and many times the ministry leaders do not know what the others are doing.

- *Competition* – In this approach each ministry leader is in a fight with the others for limited resources, stage time, favor from the senior leadership, and volunteers. In a competition mindset, lay leaders are a commodity to be held, space & facilities are not to be shared among individual ministries, and meetings are the opportunity to make your voice heard over those of the other ministry leaders. A competition mindset can be active or passive, active when leaders are openly working against one another, passive when leaders are working to protect their turf, secure budget resources, and don't see other ministry successes as team wins.

- *Confusion* – This one is hard to explain, it just is confusing. No one knows what's going on. There are no clear expectations, no one knows what the core values are, no one knows what anyone else is doing, and there's no real clarity on where a ministry fits in the overall scheme of things. It's like a football team where no one knows the play so they just kinda sorta try and figure it out. It never works.

- *Dictatorship* – A ministry staff where the senior leadership declares orders and tells the staff what to do is not a team. In a top-down leadership model, the down does whatever the top says, and there is no questioning the senior leadership's authority. A dictatorship is not a team because there is no collective goal or collaborative effort; the ministry staff is there to do the bidding of the senior leadership.

- *Nothing* – This is the tragic one, where nothing happens. There's no team because there's nothing happening. Think of the movie "The Mighty Ducks" before the coach showed up. Everyone just skated around the ice and did whatever they wanted. There's no focus, no vision, no direction, no meetings, no communication, nothing. Sadly, I think this non-team happens more than we would like to admit, as evidenced by the fact so many churches are in decline.

In a compilation, the individual elements are combined to reach a total. Count all the volunteers serving across the various ministry areas, add giving receipts for the last year, or take a quick look at the church calendar to see it full. All of these are good things, but they don't necessarily reflect a ministry team operating with a unified purpose. Compilation efforts won't always give up individual agendas for the sake of the team, and they cause us to focus on the individual ministry areas rather than the "big picture."

Collaboration looks different. Collaboration brings together individuals who are focused explicitly on one shared goal. The big picture is used to define ministry effectiveness, and this happens only within a true ministry team. Frank LaFasto and Carl Larson, experts in team building and team dynamics, note that on high-performing teams, collaboration was seen as a key ingredient to the team's success. On high performing teams, key team members were willing to put their own focus aside for the sake of improving the team's overall performance and building up other team members.[i] In a church, such collaboration could be the multiplication of small groups through the development new groups and teachers from existing groups. It could be the alignment of children and student ministries to make a coordinated effort to disciple and equip families. It could also be the decision of the leaders to put aside personality and preference for the sake of ministry effectiveness. In essence, collaboration is a shared ministry strategy that brings together various groups of people for a common goal.[ii] Collaboration also has a subjective nature, and often takes place in the way the ministry team relates to one another. Collaboration takes the form of consensus, and is evident in how team members communicate, handle conflict, or cooperate with each other's ministries.

What is a team?

If you search for books about teams on Amazon, you will find almost 185,000 results, and if you Google "teams" you will have to work through 204,000,000 results. With so many options, how can we know what a team is? Teams are made up of individual members who bring together their unique personalities, perspectives, and skill sets. Paul wrote in Galatians 3:28 "you are all one in Christ Jesus," which provides the ministry team the basis to overlook differences for the sake of Christian unity. Team members come from a variety of backgrounds, education levels, personality types, experience, ages, and ministry roles, all of which bring a unique contribution to the ministry team. Ministry teams come together with a shared calling, high character, necessary skills, and chemistry to build a healthy culture. As we look closely at what a team is and does, here are some insights from good books on teams.

Stephen Macchia, author of *Becoming a Healthy Team*, defines a ministry team as a "manageable group of diversely gifted people who hold one another accountable to serve joyfully together for the glory of God by sharing a common mission, embodying the loving message of Christ, accomplishing a meaningful ministry, and anticipating transformative results."[iii] Aubrey Malphurs, defines it as "the right people who will fulfill the mission and vision of the church," and recognizes that an effective ministry team is one of character, competence, and chemistry.[iv] The team members who are part of an effective team bring together a combination of attitude, behaviors, and skills for the benefit of the team.[v] Bill Hybels of Willow Creek Community Church writes that an effective ministry team should be selected through a criteria of character, competence, and chemistry—each of which is non-negotiable and should be sought in the stated order. Hybels believes that "a healthy and effective team member must have unwavering character, be skilled in their position and calling, and fit well with the existing team members."[vi]

Richard Hackman, a consultant writing for Harvard Business Press, notes that a real team has a team task, clear boundaries, clearly specified authority to manage their own work processes, and membership stability over some reasonable period of time.[vii] For Hackman, the leader's most important job is to "establish and maintain the handful of organizational conditions that foster and support competent teamwork."[viii] The importance for ministry teams is simple: team members know what their roles are, what their goals are, and are given the support from both the senior leadership, the governing committees, and the congregation to fulfill their calling. In the high-performing teams that Hackman observed, there was a significant amount of freedom within the team for the team members to govern themselves, but only because the foundation had been laid by the senior leadership.

Pat MacMillan, author of *The Performance Factor*, describes team leaders using terms like facilitator, networker, coach, resourcer, and boundary arranger. He also believes that their ability to lead comes from their unquestioned commitment to serve the team, rather than be served by the team.[ix] But this concept of visionary, high-competency, and influential leadership belongs in the hands of the lead pastor, who has been entrusted not only by the congregation but by God to faithfully steward and lead His church towards greater faithfulness and fruitfulness.

Patrick Lencioni, a teams consultant and author of *5 Dysfunctions of a Team*, describes healthy teams behaving in five distinct ways: trusting one another, engaging in unfiltered conflict around ideas, committing to decisions and plans of action, holding one another accountable for delivering against those plans, and focusing on the achievement of collective results.[x] For Macchia, healthy teams will trust, empower, assimilate, manage, and serve-without these, they will look more "like a poorly managed circus than a high-performing team."[xi] Malphurs draws out an important aspect of teams: They lead by consensus. Consensus is not uniformity, but it is unity around the idea, even if individual team members disagree with the decision chosen.[xii]

Lafasto and Larson describe the five conditions of an effective team: collaborative team members, relationships, group processes that foster effectiveness, good team leaders to steer the team, and an organizational environment that encourages collaboration and teamwork.[xiii] George Cladis, author of *Leading the Team Based Church*, lists covenanting, visionary, collaborative, culture creating, trusting, and empowering as attributes of a healthy ministry team which he describes as a "powerful fellowship of leaders."[xiv] Culture creating stands out from Cladis' list for this section because it is the role of the church staff (and in particular the lead pastor) to chart the course for the church by shaping the culture of the church and especially on the ministry team.

A ministry team is healthy and effective when the team members know the plan and path of the church as the visionary leadership of the lead pastor sets it out. The lead pastor sets the culture for the ministry team, lays out the mission and vision for the church, and determines the strategy and focus for the ministry team. In essence, the lead pastor functions like a head coach, who directs the operation of the team toward a common goal. This direction and strategy needs to be emphasized at every meeting, permeate the entire ministry culture, and serve as the basis for evaluation of ministries and leaders.[xv] Some team members operate like the captains on the team, who are able to take the direction of the head coach and bring that to the rest of the team. Team members serve as the catalysts among the congregation to see lasting change take place.

The definition of a ministry team we will use for this book is: *a group of ministry leaders working together to accomplish a common vision for a local congregation.* Ministry teams don't exist to maintain a list of programs, cater to preferences, or serve the personal projects or agendas of team members. An effective ministry team is made up of diverse people brought together not only by a shared focus but by a lead pastor who develops the team, sets the culture, and brings the team members together for synergy and cooperation. It also has a common vision; there is no ambiguity or uncertainty about what the vision is and how they fit into its implementation. They aren't just busy, they're productive.

In order to develop an effective ministry team, we will look at four specific areas that contribute to a team culture, the 4 C's. The four areas are Calling, Character, Competency, and Chemistry. Let's look at the implications of these four concepts in an effective ministry team:

1. An effective ministry team has a shared calling - A ministry team is built of people who have been brought together under their common story of salvation through Christ, whom God has set apart for the specific work of ministry, to "equip the saints for the work of ministry" (Ephesians 4:12), who have been recognized by a local church as being called, and who are equipped with gifts, passions, and desires for effective ministry service.

2.   An effective ministry team has <u>unquestioned character</u> - Ministry team members must be above reproach, stable in their marriage and family, trustworthy with money and confidential matters, and not enslaved by any habitual sin that might affect their ministry and the reputation of the church. Unquestioned character reflects on the testimony of the team members, and is the most important part of spiritual leadership.

3.   An effective ministry team has <u>leaders with competency</u> - Just as a baseball player needs to be able to throw and hit, an effective minister needs a certain skill set to fulfill his calling. Part of having an effective ministry team includes having talented, skilled, and growing team members. Identifying team members' skill sets and putting them in position to thrive in their strengths and grow in their weaknesses is crucial to ensuring a high level of effectiveness in serving the church.

4.   An effective ministry team has <u>good chemistry with one another</u> - Since ministry is primarily about people, those who serve on the ministry team should be good with people. Ministry teams members get along with one another, have a rapport with one another, treat one another with mutual respect, and carry themselves well in their relationships with those in authority over them and in authority under them. A pastor friend once said he would take a prospective ministry team member out for a round of golf to see how the candidate interacted with the other team members, the golf course staff, and how he handled himself during the round.

Each ministry team element has an individual and team component, which both contribute to the development of the effective ministry team. A shared calling functions as the starting point for developing an effective ministry team, as the team members have been called by God as individuals and together as a ministry team unit. Second, character holds the entire chain together for the ministry team. If it's broken, nothing else matters. Specific areas like finances, family, and integrity will be addressed because of their importance for developing an effective ministry team. Third, competency is crucial because no matter how strong a team member's call or character might be, they must be able to do their job. A survey of ministry experts helped determine the most essential competencies and qualities for ministry effectiveness. Lastly, chemistry is important because it brings together the individuals for a common goal. If we're going to work alongside people, we should at least enjoy being around them.

Reflection Questions
1.   What do you think about your church's ministry leadership? Are you a team? Or a collaboration? Or something else?

2.   Of the 4 C's, which do you think your church's leadership team is strongest with? Weakest?

3.   When was the last time you laughed with others in leadership?

Chapter 2
Calling: God Builds a Ministry Team

One of my mentors shared a story from his days as an admissions representative for a seminary. A long-haul trucker called absolutely convinced he needed to enroll, and quickly. As the rep got to know "Larry," the story got quite unusual. Larry shared that God spoke to him and said he was to be the successor to Billy Graham. My mentor's response was "you have my attention, go ahead and tell me your story of how you became a Christian, what your wife thinks about this, and what you're doing now to prepare yourself." Larry answered by saying that he wasn't a Christian and hadn't been to church in years, that he had talked about it with his live-in girlfriend/common-law wife and she was on board with it, as were their numerous illegitimate children. He continued to talk about how he was sure God had told him this was what he was to do with his life, and he needed to go to seminary to learn more about God.

Larry sounded like he might have misunderstood his calling in life, no matter his intentions or where his heart was. Understanding your calling helps you to see that you're in the right role at the right time. If we're to develop healthy ministry teams, we have to begin with team members who are absolutely confident that they are serving in a role to which they have been called. Few things are harder than serving outside of where God has clearly called and prepared you. As we talk about our calling, we'll look at it three ways: an individual's general calling to ministry, a calling to a particular church, and a calling to a ministry team. Each of these contributes to understanding how God shapes our ministry teams and those team members.

Called as Individuals

How does God call people to ministry today? Does He call like Paul and blind them on the road? Does He speak directly like Moses and the burning bush? Does He come and give unusual requests like He did to Ezekiel? Sadly, it doesn't always work out that way—there are some with very dramatic calling stories, but most of us in ministry did not experience scales falling from our eyes. Many times, God uses a variety of avenues to get our attention, we're compelled by lostness and want to do something about it, or there is an experience within the heart that points towards vocational service to God.[xvi] No matter how God calls a person, once a person is called the compelling drive of their life is to be more effective in serving Him and His Church.[xvii] Spurgeon called it "an intense, all absorbing desire for the work."[xviii]

God doesn't just call people in a vacuum, however, He uses different groups to confirm and qualify the calling of an individual. Trusted and mature Christians serve as a great barometer for a person's ministry calling and their counsel is wise for any minister or prospective minister to consider. These barometers can include other pastors in the person's life, mentors, friends, and family. If others notice spiritual gifts, a life of character, growth in their faith, passions, skills, and desires for ministry, that is a good confirmation! These trusted people can help determine if God is really calling someone to ministry or to something else. Dave Bruskas goes further to say that "a man who believes he is called to pastoral ministry must undergo serious examination by qualified pastors." This testing process, often culminating in a formal process of licensure or ordination, serves to not only sharpen a prospective ministry leader's calling but also to bless and encourage him on his lifelong journey of service to Christ and His Bride. A helpful list and explanation of ministry skills and characteristics will be discussed in chapter 4 on competency.

Every single member on the ministry team at some point in their life recognized that God was calling them to a life of service. As the coach of the ministry team, lead pastors should take time to know and understand the background and calling of the team members. It will help the pastor know how to lead them, where they come from, and what they bring to the team. This calling is part of their spiritual journey, and God is going to use their calling to accomplish great things in their lives and in the Kingdom. So their calling needs to be sharpened and shepherded; as they grow in their calling and mature in their faith, they will become more effective in their ministry. No matter how talented an athlete is, there is always room for improvement. That's why MLB players still take batting practice and get coaching for fielding ground balls. For a ministry leader, this sharpening is part of the process of growth (Romans 8, Philippians 1:3). So take the calling that your ministry team has shared and work with them to their giftedness so they can grow to become more effective ministers of the gospel. They will do the same for you if you are willing to invest in them. A shared sense of personal calling will allow for the development of the team identity.

Called to a Particular Church

Not only were the ministry leaders on your team called as individuals at some point in their lives, they were also called to the church where you serve. Players are drafted by teams who want them, believing that player will fit the team's plan, benefit the team, and help accomplish the team's goals. Remember, no one serves at your current church by accident. A process affirmed you over a number of qualified candidates, and you were tested and affirmed by a search team or congregation for your position. I believe three elements shape our understanding of being called to a particular church: culture, community, and compatibility.

A calling to a particular local church first involves the church's culture. Each church has its own individual identity that sets it apart from the thousands of other churches across the nation. The church culture includes its history (a young plant, a result of a growing suburb, or a downtown first church), its style (dress, church architecture church, worship style, preferred Bible translation, how visitors are recognized, how people join the church), its location (urban, suburban, rural, college town), and its people (highly transient area or a church with multiple generations of the same family worshipping together each Sunday). Each of these issues, and any number of other factors, go into shaping a church culture. Some churches identify themselves as Purpose-Driven, Seeker-Sensitive, Emergent, or Contemporary[xix]. Every little thing a church does in its services and through the week reveals its culture.

A calling to a particular church also involves the community around it. A church in the city of Detroit will look very different than a church in Possum Trot, Kentucky (yes, there really is a town called Possum Trot). Churches exist in diverse areas: urban, suburban, rural, small town, or college town. Even in those categories however, there are different demographics and different community identities within the same city. Each church is part of a particular community that has its own identity, values, and niche. If you were called to a church then you become a part of that community. What was it about your current community that drew you to it? Affinity for a church's culture is a great way to understand whether or not God has called you to a particular church: are you committed to loving, serving, investing in, and laboring in the community?

Lastly, a calling to a particular church involves compatibility with not only the church membership but also the existing leadership. I've watched many times where a church went after a great ministry leader, but he wasn't good for compatibility; it just didn't fit. I was part of a search once and it was very obvious that I was not the right fit with the staff and the vision of the church. I'm so glad we all agreed it wasn't going to be a good match. Compatibility is a hard thing to measure, but when it's there it's there—you're able to finish each other's sentences, you enjoy working together, and you look forward to seeing them at the store.

Called to the Ministry Team

Not only has God called you as an individual to a local church, He's called you to be a part of your current ministry team. This sense of calling may not have been active on your part—in other words you may not have gotten to pick the team members, but through the process of hiring and calling God has assembled your ministry team. He has assembled a ministry team around you that has different skills, personalities, and ministry passions. All are called to the same purpose, however. The important thing to remember is that it was God who brought you together. A calling to a particular ministry team involves a common vision, a shared burden, and a unified approach.

The common vision is set by the lead pastor and communicated to the ministry team: where the church is going and what God could do through them. It's driven by the shared calling each ministry leader has, shaped by the unique gifts and skills of the ministry team, and funneled through the lens of the lead pastor's pursuit of Christ's desires for His church.

Another way to think about the common vision is to call it a game plan. It's what informs and dictates the way decisions are made and ministry is done. In our church, we try to operate under a guiding mission statement of "building strong families in Christ" that gives us some parameters on how we operate. It's something that requires the leadership to believe in and buy into, or else chaos will result. Not every game plan or common vision is perfect. Sometimes things will change (Mike Tyson said it best that "everyone has a plan until they get punched in the mouth") and we'll have to adjust our common vision.

The shared burden is the working out of where God has called you and whom He has called you to serve. A shared burden on the ministry team is where the ministry team members recognize their call to not only serve in their "assigned" ministry areas, but that they have been called to share in the service to the whole church. Being called to a shared burden means that no one on the ministry team serves independently—everyone on the ministry team is committed to the success and effectiveness of the other ministry areas. A couple of very practical ways of applying this are cross training and cross-involvement. In cross training, other ministry leaders are aware of what is going on in ministry areas and can step in if needed. Vacations can be planned, but catching a stomach bug can't—so who will preach that morning? Cross training allows ministry leaders to be involved outside their "specialty" and provides a reliable leader if necessary.

Cross-involvement, one the other hand, is where ministry leaders are involved, in some capacity with different ministry areas. One way our church implements cross-involvement is during Vacation Bible School, where everyone serves in that ministry for that week. Another example is that we have specific people who handle pastoral care and visitor follow-up if our pastor is absent or on vacation. In all of these cases, the ministry team picks up the slack wherever it might be in order to reach our ministry objectives.

Lastly, being called to a particular ministry team involves a unified approach to ministry. The beauty of a ministry team is in its diversity, that different people can be brought together to serve the local church with their unique gifts, skills, passions, and desires. But they must be brought together under one unified approach. Without this unity, there can be a number of churches operating independent of each other under the same roof, competing against one another or even undermining one another. Instead, a unified approach to ministry begins with having the same end goal in mind. If ministries (and with that ministry leaders) are working towards different goals, the disunity will spread through the church. It won't look the same in every ministry, but each will work towards a common goal. Lead pastors must recognize their role in setting the approach by establishing and communicating the end goals that everyone on the team is on the same page working towards the same goals. This is all part of crafting the overall vision and direction for the church, and thus seeing the staff called together to accomplish that vision and direction.

Executing the Game Plan

If a ministry team has been assembled and looks great on paper, but doesn't do anything, is it really a successful team? Of course is isn't, it's like a football team that looks great getting off the bus and dressed out in their uniforms but can't run a simple handoff. For a ministry team to be effective, their emphasis has to extend beyond their calling to their execution. As we've seen, God has been the one at work assembling the ministry team at this time and for this work. At the top of the game plan is the goal: what are we setting out to do? This is something every ministry team has to answer and develop the game plan around this goal. Three parts go into executing a game plan: team meetings, practice, and game day. Let's look at those three things and how they fit in a ministry team.

1. Team Meetings - During the team meetings the strategy is developed. Meetings are where the playbook is finalized, the scouting reports are given out, and players receive feedback from the previous game. In ministry, the team-meeting phase is where the team identifies what they have been called to do. A lot of prayer, talking, and listening happens during this phase. The ministry team works through the question "What would God

have us be if we totally committed to the Great Commission?" As the lead pastor works as the coach in helping shape the strategy, it's important to recognize what gifts, abilities, and passions the ministry team and church possess. The game plan has to be built around the ministry strengths of the church or else it will prove ineffective.

2.   Practice - During practice, the game plan is rehearsed for game day. In planned phases, with many variables taken into consideration, the team works through the process of preparing for when it counts. The practice phase of the game plan execution is when the ministry team shares the burden. Thom Rainer has surveyed church expectations for ministry leaders, and found that many of them are under heavy expectations to meet a tremendous amount of needs. Sharing the burden develops the other ministry leaders to help carry the load of responsibility for the church. During practice, many teams insert a backup to a key position in case an injury happens. By delegating and preparing others, a team is not handcuffed in the event a key player is injured. Ministry teams share the burden by doing this as well, by delegating responsibilities to others on the ministry team or by equipping others to carry the load. Here's how to know what can be delegated and equipped: write down everything you do and put a mark by it if only you can do it. I suspect you won't find much that truly only you can do?

3.   Game Day - On game day, all the strategy and practice is put into action. When the team takes the field or court, it's game time. Here is where the ministry team unifies its approach. It is one thing to debate strategy during team meetings or practice, but when game time comes, everyone has to be on the same page with the same goal. Unifying the approach means that when it is time to do ministry and work towards the common vision, everyone is working towards the same goal. It means that all ministries, leaders, worship services, and church activities are working towards the same goal. This goal needs to be stated clearly, reinforced, and measured against everything the church does and promotes.

Remember, no two ministry leaders or churches will be identical in their calling and goals. The beauty of the Kingdom is that that many different kinds of churches, ministries, and leaders are brought together for Christ (1 Corinthians 12:12, 20; Romans 12:4). Every ministry team needs to find out what God has uniquely called them to, and pursue that calling. Get your clipboard out and start putting together your church's game plan!

Reflection Questions

1. Think about your community. When you drive around, do you have a genuine love and concern for people or do you just see your community as a place you live?

2. What all went into God bringing you to your current situation?

3. If you're doing this with a group, take a few minutes and discuss your individual callings.

Chapter 3
Character: The Foundation of a Ministry Team

In the summer of 1998 the nation was gripped by the chase for Roger Maris' single-season home run record. Sammy Sosa and Mark McGwire battled back and forth to see who would hit number 62 first. Finally, on September 8, a line drive over the left field wall gave the record to McGwire. The record that stood for 37 years fell, and would fall again in 2001 to Barry Bonds. In fact, number of sluggers filled the headlines with 23 players hitting more than fifty home runs during a season from 1995 until 2007.[xx] Fast-forward to December 13, 2007 and the release of the *Mitchell Report*, which detailed the rampant use of steroids and other drugs in Major League Baseball. Now those sluggers who once captured a nation's imagination were lampooned for their testimony before Congress and the shadow that hung over their on-field achievements.

Charles Barkley once made the statement "I am not a role model," trying to explain that it wasn't up to him to raise children—that was why they had parents. And I think he has a great, but incomplete, point. We shouldn't put athletes on a pedestal as a role model because we'll always be let down. At a more base level, however, we have the expectation that what we're seeing happen during the game is legit. We want to know that players aren't juiced, referees aren't being paid, and that what's happening really is an honest competition. We do the same thing when we go to a restaurant, buy a car, cast a vote for a politician, call a plumber, and hire a babysitter. We expect to receive what we were promised. This is the quality at the heart of character—Integrity.

Of all the traits necessary for ministry, character is the most important. Billy Graham famously said that "when money is lost, nothing is lost; when health is lost, something is lost; when character is lost, all is lost." The credibility for a ministry leader to make an impact on those he serves, to speak into lives affected by sin, and to be used as a vessel of grace is found in the personal character of the team member. The theme of integrity stands above the landscape of ministry, without it there is no effective ministry and no effective ministry team. In looking at character and how it relates to a ministry team we'll look through two lenses: private and public qualities. In determining what qualities were most important for effective ministry leaders, a dozen ministry experts were surveyed about what qualities they believed were most essential for ministry.

Integrity as Core

Before going into a discussion of the essential qualities for ministry character, it's important to discuss the core of character: integrity. Integrity can best be described as completeness,[xxi] where what people see of you in public is the same as who you are in private—a consistency between what you say, what you do, and who you are. No matter how many great qualities a person might have, as a ministry leader everything revolves around integrity. Paul gives us the standard for integrity in Acts 24:16 where he says he has "taken pains to ensure I have a clear conscience before God and man." Also, in 1 Timothy 3:2 ministry leaders are called to be blameless (KJV) or above reproach (NIV).

For a ministry team to be healthy and effective, it has to be built of team members who display a high level of character through a life of integrity. The expectation for every team member should be the same: nothing short of blamelessness. It's important to keep a culture of honesty on a ministry team so that we don't find ourselves in the game of hide-and-seek that so many churches play where issues of integrity are glossed over or ignored like a pink elephant no one is willing to acknowledge. Danny Akin gives six areas that guard integrity[xxii]:

1. Honesty – Tell the truth in all areas, no matter how small.

2. Opposite sex – Avoid any kind of appearance of evil, make a plan to never be alone with someone of the opposite sex, and resist places of temptation.

3. Money – Live above reproach, never directly handle money, and make sure expenses are legitimate when charged to the church.

4. Family – Be the same person at home as you are on the job.

5. Theology – Do you really believe what you teach, or are you simply telling people what they want to hear? Do you have a healthy understanding of what Scripture teaches about sin, ethics, morality, and Jesus?

6. Ministry – What kind of ministry are you pursuing, that of a shepherd or a celebrity?

Psalm 119:9 asks the question "how can a young man keep his life pure?" which carries over to an entire ministry team. The answer is profoundly simple: "by guarding it according to Your Word." A ministry team culture that is saturated with Scripture, where the Bible is the guide, where Jesus is made famous and God's Word is to be valued. A culture where leadership tactics, growth, or business principles are valued above integrity must be avoided at all costs. If we lose our integrity in ministry, we have lost, even if we have the appearance of success in the eyes of the world or our peers.

Qualities in Effective Ministry Team Members

Private qualities are those that a person demonstrates as an individual, like mental toughness in a basketball player or focus for a golfer. In ministry, these private qualities have a direct impact upon the performance and activity of a ministry leader. These qualities are found inside the ministry leader, but cannot be overlooked as essential to the overall health and ability of the leader. The qualities listed by the panel were: personal holiness, humility, spiritual maturity, intentionality, and financially stability.

Personal holiness is the first quality necessary in a team member, and the most important. A team member who is pursuing personal holiness can be trusted, not only do their job effectively but also to avoid scandal, which could bring shame on the church. Personal holiness is marked by an avoidance of sin and increased devotion to God. Team members who are living out their faith are doing what Paul advised Timothy to do in 1 Timothy 4:16, "watch your life and doctrine." The absence of holiness in a team member's life can have a ripple effect like Achan in Joshua 7, where one person's sin and deception had a devastating consequence on an entire nation. That same principle carries over to a ministry team—a lack of holiness among a team member can bring down an entire team and with it a church. It happens every time a pastor is revealed as an embezzler, an adulterer, or drug addict.

A second quality in effective ministry team members is humility. Arrogance and pride are the enemies of God in the life of the church (Proverbs 6:17, 8:13). Like uncovered sin, they can destroy a ministry team from the inside. Humility, though, is the practice of placing others before self, seeking the benefit of others, and working to elevate the team over the individual. Paul described this model for us in Philippians 2:5-11, where we see how Jesus lived out humility without abandoning confident and strong leadership among the disciples. Humility on a ministry team means sacrificing personal agendas for the sake of the church, helping with others' ministries, sharing praise for ministry wins, and elevating the platform for those with whom you serve. The beauty of this humility-driven team is that each team member is looking to build not only their team but also the other team members, and ultimately, the church itself.

The third quality for an effective team member is spiritual maturity. In essence, ministry is the overflow of the minister's personal walk with God. As a Christian grows in his or her faith, so grows ministry effectiveness. Ministry team members who are consistently growing in Christ are sharpening themselves through Bible study, prayer, journaling, fasting, and other spiritual disciplines.[xxiii] Sadly, such growth may not be as common as one would expect among ministry leaders: 70% of pastors reported only reading their Bible when preparing sermons or lessons, and only 26% of pastors reported actively participating in spiritual disciplines.[xxiv] I had a phone conversation with a pastor of a large church who shared their staff policy included a monthly "retreat" day to specifically spend time with God in prayer, Scripture reading, growth and reflection. This church also included the ministry team's spiritual growth as part of their job description—he wanted to establish a culture where ministers were refreshed, growing, and satisfied with their walk with God. Over the years, he had seen this create a healthy culture the reproduced many disciples.

Fourth, a ministry leader has to be intentional with what they do. This quality is important because ministry is an urgent work (John 9:4), and is the work of eternity as we have been given the task of shepherding and caring for people's souls. An intentional attitude is essential for ministry because there is little time to waste on things that don't matter.[xxv] A ministry leader that constantly operates without intentionality is like a ship without a rudder—it doesn't matter what you want to do, you have no way of getting there. The good news is that intentionality can be learned, and it can be improved. The best way to develop intentionality is through practicing being intentional with the help of a mentor.

The final private quality for an effective ministry team member is financial stability. Pastors are called to be effective at managing their homes and avoiding a love/obsession with money. Those two commands are interconnected to one another, as a family leader who is unable to manage personal finances cannot be entrusted with God's money. When hiring new staff members, spend the extra time and money to run a credit report—this will help show you and your search team what kind of candidate you're getting.[xxvi] For those currently on the ministry team, financial management includes both professional and personal aspects. Professionally, is the ministry team member responsibly managing the budget assigned to them by the church? If their spending is out of line, is it due to a lack of resources committed to the ministry or unnecessary spending? Personally, is the ministry team member staying out of debt and living within their means appropriate to care for their family?[xxvii]

Public qualities reveal themselves through personal interaction. Public qualities are the ones that people see most often. The public qualities listed by the panel were: a good "people person," compassion, an example as spouse and parent, and evangelistic.

The first public quality of an effective ministry leader is to be a "people person." For a ministry leader to function within a team and within the church, he must be comfortable being around and interacting with others. Ministry is not for the person who hides behind a closed door. The people dynamics of ministry may involve a counseling session, a Rotary breakfast, funerals, weddings, hospital visits, public worship, member care, evangelistic visits, and follow-up with worship service guests. The common denominator in each of those circumstances is people. People are even a factor in sermon preparation. Each sermon is delivered to particular people and must be tailored to them. Sermons aren't cookie cutter speeches; they're prepared and delivered with people in mind, even if the same text is preached in two different settings.[xxviii]

A second public quality for a ministry leader is to be compassionate with people. People are often seeking out a minister for comfort and direction when in crisis. In order to shepherd the church and have an influence over others' lives for the purpose of godliness, a heart of compassion must be apparent.[xxix] Just as Jesus had compassion on the crowds that followed Him because they were lost sheep, a ministry leader has to demonstrate compassion for the circumstances people find themselves in (even when it's their fault). This also takes the form of empathy, where a ministry leader is able to identify with and show genuine concern for what people face. Nothing can be more disruptive towards the redemptive process in a hurting person's life than a pastor who fakes caring for the people.

A third public quality for an effective ministry leader is to be an example as a spouse and parent. The panel felt this was an important quality for ministry because, unlike other professions, effective ministry is rooted in how the ministry leader leads and shepherds his family. This doesn't mean that a ministry leader needs to have a Stepford wife or robot children who never misbehave, but it does mean that a ministry leader is winning at home before winning at church. Ephesians 5:22-6:4 gives a helpful prescription for the family with specific instructions for wives, husbands, and children. In short, husbands are to cherish their wives and serve them in a way that reflects Christ's love and service to the church, wives are to graciously follow their husband's leadership, and children are to obey their parents. Parents are also commanded to raise their children in the Lord, but not to provoke them to anger or bitterness.

The final public quality for an effective ministry leader is to be evangelistic. A ministry team member must be concerned about those beyond the church walls, and actively pursue a response to the gospel from them. Beyond the task of personal witness is the mindset that the mission of the church is for those who are not yet a part of it, rather than for the preferences and comfort of those who are members. An effective ministry team recognizes that until every knee bows and every tongue confesses Christ (Philippians 2:10-11), there is still work to be done. This passion for the unreached, unchurched, and unengaged will carry over to the church body, which can then be mobilized for missions in their neighborhoods and among the nations. A climate on the ministry leadership team that is evangelistic sets the tone and culture throughout the church.

I want to propose six low cost but high reward ways to help build a culture of character on your ministry team. Each of these ways contribute to developing a culture that values integrity and character in ministry team members, and takes seriously the need to protect that in a fallen world where the battle is against an enemy who wants to destroy the Church (Ephesians 6:12). Taking steps to implement them will help build stronger ministry leaders, families, and churches. It will also protects the reputation of the church and its ministry leaders within the congregation and among the watching world.

1. Accountability Relationships - Proverbs 27:17 tells us that as iron sharpens iron one man sharpens another, and Ecclesiastes 4:12 that a cord of three strands is not easily broken. An accountability relationship does more than provide a coffee shop confessional; it provides the opportunity for two (or more) people to grow together and mature in their walk as a Christian, spouse, parent, and ministry leader. Some basic principles to work through when developing an accountability relationship are to engage with someone of the same sex, to make it consistent, to be intentional about why you're meeting, to be honest and transparent, and to work toward something. A forest fire starts with a spark that could be quickly extinguished, and in the same way accountability relationships help shape the character of a Christian before a tragic fall into sin happens.

2. Monitoring Software - Inexpensive software options are available that block inappropriate sites from access, provide a list of web history to a particular accountability partner, or filter

content viewed on a website.[xxx] Stories abound of pastors caught up in pornography, and we mustn't be too naive to presume that our churches and our ministry teams are immune. These filters should be put on all computers used by ministry team members, and should be set up by someone outside the ministry team who knows the passwords and ability to unlock the software. Protecting the integrity of ministry staff should be a priority for a church to consider, and software assistance provides an extra safeguard.

3. Policy and Procedure - One way to protect the character of a ministry team is to remove any barriers that might lead to even the appearance of evil (1 Thessalonians 5:22). Revisit your church's policy structure, whether it's formally adopted or informally understood, and look to see if there are any loopholes or areas of revision. For example: Do you allow your youth ministry leaders to be in the car alone with a teen of the opposite sex? Is the office door open (or a window open) when you are counseling?[xxxi] By developing policy and procedure that ensure the protection of the ministry team's character, you are allowing the ministry team more freedom to serve the church and counsel people through difficult situations. I believe that a church that is up front about its policy and procedure to protect the integrity and witness of its ministry team is a church that is committed to gospel ministry in all areas and is willing to live and serve above reproach.

4. Team Devotions - As a team, make devotions a regular part of your meetings. Don't merely get bogged down in the details of programming, activities, calendars, and lists; take the time to focus on the Word, prayer, and carrying one another. Rotate the responsibility of leading this devotional time. These devotions can be from a devotional book, or from the individual's own study and reflection—the key is that these are times to shape and grow the ministry team members' character and Christlikeness. This also encourages the ministry team members to read good books and dive into the Word, which helps shape their character.

5. Performance Reviews - During my dissertation study, I interviewed a church that made personal character a part of each ministry team member's employment evaluation. Each ministry team member was expected to grow in their walk, making investments in their family, and in an accountability relationship. These annual reviews provided a way for the church to not only hold their ministry staff to a high standard of performance in their jobs, but also to recognize how important their character, integrity, and personal growth was. The purpose

of including this in an employee's review isn't to create an unnecessary burden, but to show how important the link between home and church is for an effective, transformational, long-lasting ministry.

6. Marriage Investments - The website *PastorBurnout.com* paints a bleak picture of what ministry looks like for the family. In many families, the work of ministry creates a barrier between husband and wife, which leads to a number of ministry leaders going through a divorce, addiction, or adulterous relationship. Making marriage investments with the ministry team can provide an easy way for couples to reconnect, rest, and renew their commitment to one another. Some easy ways to make these investments are to cultivate a culture of prayer for ministry team members and their families, to offer ministry team leaders a date night with their spouse by watching the kids, or to develop a personnel policy that allows ministry team leaders to attend a marriage enrichment conference/event.

I hope you're seeing how important character is for effective ministry teams, and how important it is to develop a culture that values, builds, and cultivates character.

Reflection Questions
1. How much emphasis does your church and leadership put on personal character?

2. What are some ways you can intentionally build and develop character in leadership team members?

3. What policy & procedure changes do you need to make to protect character?

Chapter 4
Competency: Skills for a Ministry Team

Every sport has a certain set of competencies or skills that are necessary in order to play. In basketball it's necessary to be able to dribble, shoot, and run. In soccer one must be able to run, kick, and keep your hands off the ball. In tennis one must be able to serve, return, and volley. Baseball even refers to exceptionally skilled players as "Five Tool" players, who are able to throw, run, field, hit for average, and hit for power. We love the stories of athletes who "break the mold," and succeed because of their grit or willpower in the absence of overwhelming skills. Everyone loves the movie *Rudy* because he played for Notre Dame despite being undersized and underskilled. Unfortunately, those stories are the exception rather than the norm, because of how important fundamental skills are for athletic success.

The main idea of this chapter is that effective ministry team members need to have a solid foundation of ministry skills—the observable actions or behaviors in the work of ministry. These skills, in connection with the character traits listed in the previous chapter, provide the structure for an effective ministry team member. It's important for a ministry team member to be able to do what they have been called to do. Combining members' skill sets allows more to be accomplished by the team. The skills in this chapter serve as a baseline for what is necessary, in the opinion of the aforementioned ministry panel, for being an effective ministry team member. The great news with all of these skills is that they can all be learned, acquired, developed, evaluated, and improved. There are three categories of skills necessary to be an effective ministry team member: personal, pastoral, and interpersonal.

Personal skills primarily involve just the team member, though a ripple effect is also there for each skill. These are similar to the private qualities in chapter 3. In sports, personal skills might be the off-field preparation a player does to be ready for a game, like private workouts or off-season conditioning.

The first personal skill from the panel is time management.[xxxii] Few churches use a tracking system like time cards, but every church has an expectation for how time is used. Without effective skills in time management, a ministry leader will be in trouble. One pastor said it this way, "There's no escaping it, Sunday will always come." Time management is possible through blocking time—building the workday around time slots with specific assignments during those blocks.[xxxiii] Here's a sample of what a blocked day might look like in ministry[xxxiv]:

8:00-8:15	Check phone messages	12:00-1:00	Lunch with wife
8:15-8:30	Check & respond to email	1:00-2:30	Staff meeting
8:30-9:30	Sermon prep	2:30-2:45	Check & respond to email
9:30-9:45	Check in with ministry team members	2:45-3:00	Coffee break
9:45-10:00	Make shut-in phone calls	3:00-4:00	Counseling appointment
10:00-10:30	Return phone messages	4:00-5:00	Counseling appointment
10:30-11:30	Counseling appointment	5:00-5:15	Check & respond to email
11:30-12:00	New member orientation prep	5:15-5:30	Write out daily plan for tomorrow

The second personal skill is prioritizing, which is the practice of identifying and doing things based on their importance and urgency.[xxxv] Not everything in church life demands an immediate response or action.[xxxvi] The Rainer Group found that effective pastors focused on making sure things got done without being the one to do it all.[xxxvii] Perhaps the most important thing to learn in prioritizing is to say the word "no." An effective ministry team member has to recognize what is most important, most urgent, most necessary, and graciously say no to the rest. Pat Lencioni, author and teams consultant, once said, "If everything is important, nothing is important." In Acts 6, the Apostles stated their intention to do a few things well, and by doing so gave priority to their calling. A ministry team member can be more effective in their work and build the team dynamic by effectively making priorities of what is important, and blocking time to accomplish those things. A helpful way to learn to prioritize is to make a daily or weekly checklist of what needs to be accomplished, with a priority rank assigned to each task.

Daily Activity	Priority	Weekly Activity	Priority
Return visitors with phone calls	1	Prepare sermons - Sunday AM & PM	1
Make hospital visit	2	Staff evaluations	3
Call John about joining Sunday	2	Go over order of worship with staff team	1
Email deacons	3	Review Sunday bulletin	2
Write article for church website about sermon	2		

The final personal skill is financial management. Few people will ever see the inside of a ministry leader's checkbook, but the effect of that ledger can be felt throughout the church—personal financial practices are directly related to church finances. The ability to design, implement, and live on a budget is crucial.[xxxviii] The financial decisions made by team members directly affect the others— for example, if one member overspends, it means less resources for the other ministry areas.[xxxix] Financial management is extra important because giving in most churches has declined. Look for ways to be more effective with ministry resources, collaborate with other churches for sharing VBS supplies, and pray for God to create a culture of generosity in the church.

Pastoral skills are the skills a ministry leader has to use in order to fulfill the "church side" of their role, regardless of job description. Every ministry leader, whether a lead pastor or preschool minister, will need to develop and use these skills. The pastoral skills identified by the ministry panel were: teaching & applying the Bible, disciple and equip, and counsel believers in crisis.

Perhaps the most important skill identified was the ability of a ministry team member to teach & apply the Bible to life. Teaching the Bible can happen in a variety of settings (pulpit, small group, children's church), but it has to be more than presenting facts or theology trivia. Teaching the Bible effectively means that a ministry leader is able to connect the Bible to people's lives, seeing Romans 12:1-2 transformation happening as minds are renewed in Christ. That's the goal of teaching the Bible, whatever the context. This is the point Gary Bredfeldt, a pastor and seminary professor, makes in his book *Great Leader Great Teacher*, where he says that all other ministry responsibility comes from the outflow of the teaching ministry.[xl] I want to propose 5 questions to ask when teaching the Bible in any setting:

1. **What is the point?** – There should be one major driving idea behind the lesson or sermon. I call it the "Big Main Idea," and others might call it the "Sermon in a Sentence," or something to that effect.

2. **What is your goal?** – What do you want the outcome to be? It doesn't have to be earth-shattering, but you need to have a goal. It can be as simple as "for the youth group to love their Bible" or as complex as "I want to cast a comprehensive vision for implementing an Acts 1:8 missions strategy."

3. **Who is your audience?** – A skilled Bible teacher knows that the heart of the message won't change, but how that message is delivered will. Sometimes we have great content, great transitions, and great introductions, but our lesson wasn't delivered in a way that resonated with the audience.

4. **How are you getting there?** – A well-crafted outline serves as the map towards achieving the end result. The outline shapes the lesson or sermon, and can help the audience to follow where you're going. This is not the place for "vacation shortcuts" where you end up on a tangent.

5. **How is your takeoff and landing?** - When we fly, we remember takeoff and landing because they are tension moments, our heartbeat picks up and we're more alert. Those are the introduction and conclusion for any lesson. Everything else is cruising altitude; it's important and essential to get to the landing, but what you say first and what you say last will stick.

The second necessary pastoral skill is the ability to disciple and equip believers. Ephesians 4 identifies this skill as a necessary element to ministry and the reason why God sets apart some for ministry: to equip the saints. Discipling and equipping believers for ministry involves the work of intentionally investing in them through teaching, training, empowering, and releasing. The aim of discipling and equipping believers is to see them mature in Christ (Colossians 1:28). In this skill set, ministry is multiplied as leaders invest in others who carry on the work, who then continue the cycle of investment and training in others. Here are four steps in the discipleship and equipping process to use:

1. Identify – Sometimes a catalyst for ministry will seek out a leader's help, but many times it requires the initiative of the ministry leader.[xli] People who are identified for this might not be the most obvious choices, so it's important for a ministry leader to know people and make relationships with them.

2. Invest – As the relationship develops, a leader invests in someone by allowing them to shadow, giving increased responsibility, asking questions, giving room to learn and make mistakes, and finding their passion.[xlii]

3. Release – When I learned to ride a bike my dad stayed with me to learn how to pedal, brake, steer, and stay upright…until he decided it was time to let go. The same principle applies in discipling and equipping a Christian. At some point there will be a release, where a believer has been prepared to a point where they can handle the responsibility on their own.

4. Repeat – The disciple-making process has only begun. Now the leader and the recent disciple can repeat the process and identify the next person in whom they will invest.

The final pastoral skill for effective team ministry is the ability to provide counsel for struggling believers. Every ministry leader is in a position of trust and influence with others. Ministry leaders must be careful to work within their comfort and competency limits and not be afraid to refer a believer to a professional Christian counselor.[xliii] The important thing to remember in any counseling situation is to point people to Christ as their only hope, whether it's a deacon's crumbling marriage or a girl in the youth group whose frenemy is starting rumors.

The final category of public ministry skills is *interpersonal skills*. These are the skills important for anyone working with people. The church is an organization in which ministry team leaders need to be able to effectively deal with people. Both the interpersonal and pastoral skill sets serve to complement and add to one another. The interpersonal skills the ministry panel identified were: conflict management, delegation, leadership, administration, team building, and clear communication.

Conflict management is the first interpersonal skill essential for effective team ministry. Any time people are together conflict is inevitable, whether it's personality differences or disagreement over strategy. Peacemaker Ministries sees conflict management and peace as an outflow of the gospel.[xliv] The important thing about conflict management is that it's about reconciliation and redemption, not winning or proving a point. A ministry team member who is unable to deal effectively with conflict, who throws gas on a fire rather than water, will have a ripple effect through the church. Great news! Conflict management can be learned. Bad news. Learning conflict management happens through conflict. Part of the ministry team dynamic is that team members can help one another through conflict management, especially those who have been there before. Here are five principles to keep in mind for conflict management.

1. Keep peace, reconciliation, and redemption as the goal. Conflict management isn't about being right or getting your way, it's about God's people living in peace.

2. Maintain your integrity. Nothing can destroy a ministry leader's ability to work with people than for their integrity to be lost in a conflict.

3. Point to the gospel. The gospel serves as the best example of conflict management in Scripture. Saturate conversations in conflict management with references to the gospel.

4. Celebrate reconciliation. In Luke 15, three parables are used, and each includes a celebration that what was lost had been found. We should do the same with conflict management, to celebrate and recognize when reconciliation has happened.

5. Know when to walk away - Sometimes in conflict management we may do all we can to seek peace and reconciliation, but are dealing with someone who just wants to be mad and disgruntled. At some point, walking away isn't such a bad idea.

Delegation is the second interpersonal skill for effective team ministry. Delegation is the ability to develop and hand off ministries and projects to qualified volunteers or other staff members, which is different from dumping. Dumping occurs when a leader gives a task or drops a project on someone without coaching, accountability, motivation, or investment. Delegation, on the other hand, is the skill of raising up someone else by discipling and equipping him or her so they can be trusted to take on ministry responsibility on their own. In delegation, a leader raises up others; in dumping the leader keeps others low. Delegation multiplies the effectiveness of a ministry team because it frees up the time and energy for the ministry team to focus on their calling and the big picture. It also brings others into the process to give them a sense of ownership and value in the ministry—making them producers instead of just consumers.

Leadership is an underestimated important skill for effective ministry team members. Just because someone has a position does not necessarily make him or her a leader. Leadership only happens when someone follows, which makes leadership more about influence than anything else.[xlv] Leadership is a skill rather than part of character because leadership can be learned. Leadership occurs when a ministry team member has a captivating vision or goal, communicates it to others, and influences them to follow.[xlvi] Leadership also involves the willingness of the team member to do what is necessary and to be willing to go where he wants to influence followers to go. For example, if a youth pastor wants to lead his students to be missions-focused, but fails to actually engage in such missions-focused service, he will have less influence than if he were consistently modeling such behaviors. Leadership requires a ministry team member to go first, tell others why it's wonderful, and encourage the others to join.

Administration is the management side of interpersonal skills. Leadership is where the team member seeks to cast influence, but administration is where the leader puts the vision into practice. A sports analogy could be where a coach is a phenomenal recruiter who is able to bring the best players to the school because they believe in what he says. A coach, however, must be able to manage the game and effectively use the roster to win games. Baseball provides a great example of the need for administrative giftedness and skill, when a manager brings in the right pitcher to face a key batter, arranges the lineup built around players' strengths and contributions. Additionally a great manager will defers praise to the players when things go well, but will "own" the team's failures as his own rather than pass the blame.

Administration on a ministry team involves the skill of making sure that everything that goes into the life of the church is staffed, prepared, ready, and functioning at the proper time. Administration is interpersonal because it involves the placement, preparation, and contribution of people. It also is interpersonal because for many ministry team leaders, it can be an overwhelming task that requires additional help in the form of paid staff, volunteers, or interns who are able to manage the workflow and people necessary to pull off a ministry.

Another interpersonal skill identified for effective ministry team members is the ability to build a team. Team building is important for ministry because there is too much work for any one person to complete, no matter how brilliant or gifted the leader might be. Just like a team has to be built among the ministry team for it to be effective in the church, ministry team members need to be able to build a team around their ministries. Recruiting team members, training them, empowering them, and playing to their strengths are ways to develop a team. Playing to strengths occurs when a leader recognizes an individual what team member's skills and insures those skills are maximized in ministry.

Deploying team members is as important as recruiting or coaching them. If team members are consistently out of their areas of strength, passion, and giftedness, it will have a crippling effect on a team. Tom Brady does not need to run the option. The extroverts on your team don't need to be on the setup crew for events. If a leader has recruited good people, prepared them, and put them in a position to use their strengths, little oversight or intervention may be necessary. Just let them go!

The final interpersonal skill is to clear communication. In church ministry, a leader needs to be able to communicate effectively in a few different ways: writing, public speaking, social media, conversations, small groups, and non-verbal communication. If a leader is to be effective, he must be able to get the message out in such a way that people receive it, understand it, and embrace it. Three words to remember when communicating are: concise, clear, and consistent. Is what you're trying to say concise enough that the message isn't lost in the shuffle? Is what you're trying to say obvious in your communication? Is what you're trying to say reinforced through several avenues?

Application – Practicing for Ministry

Just as a sports team has to practice the fundamentals and skills necessary to play, it would be wise and helpful for ministry leaders to develop ministry skills through some of the same principles that coaches use to shape practices.

1. Identify your strengths and weaknesses. In what areas of ministry skill to you excel? Have others give you an honest assessment to make sure that you're getting an accurate picture. One thing a coach does during practice is work on weaknesses to improve them.

2. Run through scenarios. Football teams practice through a variety of scenarios, including injuries to key players, so that when the game takes place, they have a plan and are prepared for any number of factors. On the worksheet you'll find a list of potential scenarios to discuss as a ministry team.

3. Use role-playing situations. This approach is especially helpful with the public skills (pastoral and interpersonal) listed in this chapter. If your ministry team has young men who want to preach, give them opportunity to preach short sermons as devotions with the ministry team. Practice common conflict management issues. The important thing is that these situations be instructive and helpful.

4. Give feedback and provide evaluation. It doesn't matter how much a team practices if they never get feedback on their performance. The lead pastor's role in this principle is to give timely and constructive feedback to team members' skill development.

5. Always look for improvement. No matter how long you've been in ministry, there will be places to improve to be more effective. Continually ask questions, sharpen your skills, and keep working on them.

Reflection Questions

1. What are some competencies in your ministry you'd like to sharpen or improve?
2. Can you write down the names of some coaches, denominational resources, or other help who could be an asset to your leadership team?
3. Why do you think administration is so important for a ministry leader?

Chapter 5
Chemistry: A Ministry Team Comes Together

The 2013 Boston Red Sox won their third World Series in 10 years, which was magnified by the abysmal failure of the previous season. The 2012 Red Sox were loaded with talent but produced their worst record since 1965 and finished last in their division. The problem? One word: chemistry. Bruce Katcher noted that the 2012 Red Sox were filled with negative players, an ego-driven manager who didn't get along with his assistant coaches, and a toxic relationship between the team and the front office.[xlvii] The 2013 Red Sox were the complete opposite of their predecessors. Not only did the 2013 Red Sox have talent, their influx of new players were known for being good influences in the clubhouse, and the negative players from the season before were traded away. Unlike the ego of the previous manager, the 2013 manager worked well with the assistant coaches, the players, and the front office. The team executives were more in touch with the pulse of the locker room and worked to build a relationship between the office and the locker room. Red Sox management credited these factors for their 2013 success.[xlviii]

What do church ministry and a Major League Baseball team have in common? Relationships within the team will determine the success and effectiveness of the team, as much as, if not more so than, the team members' skills. Good chemistry within a ministry team can be the catalyst for an incredibly fruitful season of ministry, and bad chemistry can be the cancer that destroys not only a staff, but also a church, from within. A ministry team can have a sense of calling both individually and as a team, a roster of high character leaders who have proven themselves faithful, and possess a skill set that can tackle the impossible. But, without team chemistry to create a synergistic relationship between the team members, the end result can be a fractured staff and a divided church. Healthy and solid relationships within the ministry team can multiply a church's ministry effectiveness across the board with a healthy rapport among the leaders. Why is chemistry so important? I want to suggest three ways chemistry is vital in local church ministry.

1. Ministry is Personal –   Systems are important in ministry because they set the course for how ministry is done, but systems, strategies, initiatives, and programs don't fully encompass ministry. Ministry is the constant interaction of people, phone calls, meetings, counseling appointments, collaboration, hospital visits, meetings, and more meetings.

Because a ministry team is going to have so much interaction with one another it's important to have a solid chemistry between the team members. Developing good chemistry makes meetings more engaging, creates more rapport, opens up avenues of honesty and transparency, and fosters an environment of trust. A 2011 study even found that enjoying work relationships has positive health benefits, likely from the removal of unnecessary stress in the workplace.[xlix]

2. The Body Connects and Intersects – Ministries in the church don't happen in isolation from one another, no matter how hard a church might try. The best predictor of a growing student ministry usually is a thriving children's ministry. The strength of a church's deacons will be largely connected to its men's ministry. There is a trickle-down effect of chemistry within the ministry team throughout the layers of the church. A ministry team with good chemistry will carry on the synergy of healthy relationships and effectiveness to the volunteers who serve in other ministries, especially the volunteers who serve in multiple ministry areas. As chemistry flourishes it strengthens lay leadership in all areas of ministry. It all starts with how the ministry team leaders relate to one another. There is no way to remove the interconnectedness of the body of Christ, where each part affects the others (Romans 12:4, 1 Corinthians 12).

3. Ministry is Hard – Burnout is a common theme in ministry as Leadership Resources pointed out in a 2013 article.[l] Burnout can come from draining relationships, church conflict, inadequate preparation for the grind of ministry, or from the cumulative effects of stress. Because ministry is hard, it is imperative to have good relationships and good chemistry with the other members of your ministry team. Several years ago, a church I knew of went through some painful but necessary

    changes that dramatically affected the church's culture and dealt with issues that had festered for decades. When I talked to the executive pastor about this situation and asked how they survived, he responded by saying "we knew it was going to be hard, but we went into it as a band of brothers." Because the ministry team had great relationships, mutual support, trust in the lead pastor, and enjoyed working together, they were able to weather a difficult season and come out on the other side more effective in ministry.

What does chemistry look like?
    What does chemistry on a ministry team look like? A social media survey produced a variety of responses from both pastors

and laypeople. One person described team chemistry as "not always having to agree on everything but committing together to a common purpose." Another said "friends working on something big together," while a career counselor said "respect between members, pride is out the window, recognizing and deferring confidently to each other's giftedness, and when you can give bad news but not hurt feelings." A lead pastor described his dream of team chemistry boiled down to friendships, unity, and trust. For this pastor, accomplishments on the staff were directly related to their chemistry and unity on the team. I'm going to use his three characteristics to describe what chemistry on a ministry team looks like.

First, chemistry looks like friendships. Friendships are a big deal among coworkers because of the personal and professional support network that can form from them.[li] This takes the ministry environment beyond getting through to the next Sunday or checking off the task list. Instead, it becomes an environment with personal

interest in each other as more than co-workers. It doesn't have to be within an office, it can be over group text or social media or in other non-physical communication. In order to know if you have a true friendship on the ministry team, ask yourself a simple question: "If I didn't have to work with this person, would I still want to be around them?" Friendships on the team allow for help with problems with kids at home, support during difficult times, and celebrating big things in the lives of each team member. Friendships lead to chemistry because they open the pathway to people doing real, meaningful, personal, family-intensive, and Kingdom-lasting work *together.* Friendships on a ministry team give people a reason to come into work, because they know they'll enjoy who they'll be around and will look forward to seeing them.

Second, chemistry looks like unity. Unity is a big deal because it was so often what Jesus and Paul prayed for in the local church (1 Corinthians 1:10, John 17:20-23, Ephesians 4:3). For a leadership team, unity is not uniformity—unity is where the team is on the same page and focused on the same objective, uniformity is like penguins, where there is no way to tell anyone apart. God hasn't called everyone to be identical, because we all benefit from diversity in the Body (1 Corinthians 12, Romans 12). But there needs to be clarity and agreement on the "big deal" issues, such as the gospel and the vision/mission of the church—these are the non-negotiables of a team approach to ministry.

Unity on a ministry team is a lot like parenting—behind closed doors there is freedom to discuss and even to disagree, but once the door is open everyone is in agreement on the course of action. The beauty is that, like a married couple that is committed to and loves one another, these kinds of discussions and agreements are easier because of the relational capital that has been built up through the pursuit of real friendship with the other team members. Dave Ramsey's EntreLeader website offers five killers of team unity[lii], and the opposites of those provide insights into what unity on a team looks like and does. Unity on a ministry is reflected in:

1. Communication – Are there clear and effective communication patterns and channels on the team?

2. Confidentiality – Can team members be trusted with sensitive information and not gossip?

3. Conflict resolution – Conflict isn't bad, but avoiding resolving it is. A team with unity knows how to handle things to bring people back together

4. Common purpose – A unified team is heading the same direction on a clear path to get there

5. Clear expectations – The unified team knows that excellence is expected of them

Third, chemistry looks like trust. No matter how close a team might be personally, or how much unity they have around a common vision or strategy, if there's not trust there will never be chemistry. Trust is the understanding, and expectation that the team members will have each other's backs. How important is trust? Nan Russell at Psychology Today refers to trust as the "new workplace currency,"[liii] and Cuddy, Kohut, and Neffinger at *Harvest Business Review* claim that trust is the entryway to effective leadership and influence.[liv] Without trust on a ministry team, it will be impossible to make significant accomplishments as a team—it's not to say individual members won't make significant accomplishments, but the potential from a collective, unified, and cohesive team effort will be lost. Trust is a lengthy asset to earn, and comes as a result of intentionally seeking to build trust in and receive trust from the other team members. This can happen through difficult times, team members buying into and helping each other on their ministry assignments (pastors, this may mean taking a pie to the face at VBS), and taking time to talk about life outside the office.

How is chemistry created?

But the biggest question after "what" is "how," because it's very easy to describe what chemistry on a ministry team looks like. The rubber meets the road when you ask how chemistry happens on a ministry team. It's not as simple as mixing two people in an office setting and hope that a reaction happens—if it were that easy we wouldn't see so many churches and ministry teams operating without synergy, focus, and teamwork. There are four ways I believe chemistry happens on a ministry team. They're within reach, but they all require a level of commitment from team members, and especially from the lead pastor, because he is the point person responsible for developing team chemistry. It's up to the team members to determine how much they will buy in to team chemistry, but the climate of the ministry team is set by the lead pastor. Part of being the primary leader of the ministry team requires that the lead pastor must model these four ways, and work to instill them into the DNA of the ministry team.

First, and most importantly, chemistry happens intentionally. One summer I was too busy and overwhelmed. We were adjusting to life with a baby, I was in the middle of doctoral work, and was serving full-time as a youth. That spring we had painstakingly worked on our landscaping by clearing weeds, laying mulch, replanting shrubs, and digging up dead bushes. My yard looked great. After a summer of giving my yard little attention, however, it once again looked like a jungle. What was missing? I wasn't intentional about caring for the landscaping. A lack of intentional lawn care always creates an environment where weeds flourish. The same principle applies in ministry.

Chemistry is only created if the team members intentionally work toward it. Perhaps the best way to intentionally develop chemistry is to avoid isolation. If the other leadership is around the office, get out and spend time with them. If they're remote or volunteer, engage them regularly digitally. For lead pastors, sermon preparation is the most important part of their weekly schedule, *but it's not the only part*. Team chemistry won't happen if you never cross paths, even in a group text. Remember, you're not just coworkers, you're partners in Kingdom work. Carve out time every week in your schedule to interact with the other members on your ministry team.

Second, chemistry is created in crisis, when the resolve of a team is put to test. Lead pastors, if you want to see your staff come together, stand up for them to divisive or complaining church members. Crisis also forces people to work together who may not before. At the end of a crisis, team members can come out with a renewed sense of purpose, unity, and resolve. This very thing happened to me a few years ago when I was forced to endure a very difficult season in ministry, when the right thing to do proved costly. Out of that experience of crisis, I developed a whole new appreciation for and rapport with several others on the ministry team. Those relationships remain strong today, and I credit a lot of it to that crisis episode. Few championship teams go through a season unscathed and we shouldn't expect anything different in ministry.

Unlike intentionality, crisis moments aren't things that can be planned or scheduled into your weekly agenda. Chemistry grows through crisis because it causes us to react and respond. It will be difficult to develop chemistry in the midst of crisis, however, if your team hasn't built up some credit beforehand. A ministry whose members have avoided each other and failed to develop friendships during normal seasons of ministry, will struggle to come together when the crisis hits. Even though crisis-built chemistry is reactive, it still depends on an intentional focus by all the ministry team members.

Third, chemistry happens through daily interactions among the team members. This development works in conjunction with the intentionality of the team members. Hanging out or making small talk isn't enough to develop chemistry between team members. Chemistry development can happen, however, through unscripted, unplanned interactions with one another. Rather than trying to build chemistry through meetings, off-site retreats, and awkward lunches, take the opportunity to develop chemistry in the small moments. These daily interactions to develop chemistry are the moments in the hallway, at the copier, helping with each other's ministry projects, or in each other's offices. Daily interactions are spontaneous, but if they will develop chemistry they must be intentional. That cannot be emphasized enough.

Here are five ways for a lead pastor to develop chemistry in daily interactions within the ministry team:

1. Once a day engage in a conversation with a different team member about their life in ministry and at home. It can be as simple as a text message or a drop-in, or it can be part of a scheduled meeting. Regardless of *how* it happens, it's important *that* it happens.

2. Develop a "daily check-in" with ministry team members. Check-ins should be brief but they allow for a lead pastor to know what's going on in others' ministries and in the team

member's lives. This time is crucial for These daily check-ins are short but allow for the lead pastor to know what's going on in the team members' lives, and give the team member to have face time with the lead pastor.

3. Pray for each other in the office. I knew a pastor who made it regular practice to pray with all the ministry team members when he first came in the office. Eventually, some on the ministry team began praying with him as well.

4. Serve together behind the scenes. Most of what happens on a typical Sunday is planned and prepared during the week. Use this time to offer help to the music minister who's setting up for a lengthy practice, put together the children's church handouts, or make the Sam's Club run for preschool snacks with the children's team.

5. Leave the door open. It's impossible to develop chemistry if the door to your office is always closed. Developing chemistry happens as people have access. By shutting yourself off to all contact with the other team members, you're shutting yourself away from conversations that can build a real sense of chemistry.

Finally, chemistry happens when teams have fun. Google makes this part of their office culture with silly hats for new employees, nap rooms, recreation areas, and more. Perhaps the church shouldn't go quite as far as Google, but there shouldn't be a sense of dread when entering the office. Relationships on a ministry team should be fun, and the fun that comes from enjoying the people you work with leads to a growing chemistry on the team. It's important to discuss strategy, to plan events, set goals, and collaborate on the weekly grind between Sundays, because a ministry team needs to be productive. It also is important for a ministry team to be able to laugh together, enjoy their work environment, and feel free to bring appropriate humor to the table.

At the end of the day, developing chemistry on the team is something that will take an investment of time and energy. It won't be enough to be cordial or civil with one another—that will only take a team to a certain point, because cordiality is not chemistry. The role of the lead pastor cannot be emphasized enough in developing team chemistry. He is the catalyst, and his example and initiative will set the pace for the rest of the ministry team. But the best part about team chemistry is that it will lead to a team who is together— and that payoff will carry a team through anything.

Reflection Questions

1. How is your team's chemistry? Is it made of Friendships, Unity, and Trust?

2. What are some ways you can, even if you're not a lead pastor, help develop chemistry in the leadership?

3. Where do you spend your time when you're engaged in work, alone all the time or do you try to spend time with other leaders?

Chapter 6
Hiring: Assembling a Ministry Team

Draft day is the chance for a professional sports team to select the college players who will build the future of the team. Before the draft, an extensive period of interviews, evaluations, scouting, and background analysis happens. The best example of this analysis is the annual NFL Combine in Indianapolis. Each year, hundreds of potential NFL players gather to be interviewed, run the 40-yard dash, bench press, jump, throw, and catch. The goal of the combine is to identify the key players who can be selected to make an impact for several years with the team. The combine is the deciding point for many teams on whether or not to take a player. In several instances in recent years a player's draft stock has plummeted because of poor performance at the combine, getting caught with drugs, showing up unprepared for interviews, or failing a physical exam.

For a church, the opportunity to develop an effective ministry team can happen through the hiring process. Lead pastors who come in with a ministry philosophy and vision must take the time and effort to build the existing team, and help change the culture. When a position opens up that has to be filled, however, it can provide an immediate opportunity for a lead pastor to shape the ministry team toward a unified vision. Hiring new staff allows for a fresh start with team members, who are free from baggage and history. It also allows the incoming staff to fit into the paradigm set by the lead pastor. When hiring new staff, the lead pastor gets the opportunity to bring on staff members to the existing ministry team who will increase the team's ability to effectively minister in the church and in the community.

Developing an effective ministry team through the hiring process can be divided into four primary categories. This chapter will focus on team members who are not the lead pastor, but function in associate or "second chair" roles. At the end we will devote some time to discussing issues related to hiring a lead

pastor, which is a little different in its application than hiring "second

chair" leaders. Remember, developing a ministry team through hiring outside staff is often a collaborative process between church lay leadership, the lead pastor, and the existing staff. Each category in the development of a ministry team needs to be considered in order to ascertain what a prospective candidate profile looks like, and who ultimately is hired to fill a position on the church ministry team.

Calling and Hiring

Whenever hiring for a role on a ministry team, it's vital to know if the person being considered can articulate their calling to ministry. As we talked about in chapter 2, God doesn't call people in a vacuum. There is an inward, personal call where an individual senses that God is prompting them in the direction of vocational ministry. But that personal call is confirmed by other believers and finally by a local congregation. And the call extends beyond that, because God also calls individuals to particular settings, in this case potentially your church. That's why it's so important to do homework on the front end of the process of hiring a ministry team member.

First, get the potential team member's sense of calling. In the informal part of the hiring process, have the person share how they understand God's active work in their life, particularly what steered them towards vocational ministry. Ask about mentors and other godly leaders who helped that person shape their calling, and what role their "home church" had in the process. Second, have them share why they feel God may be bringing them to your particular setting. What circumstances, devotional reflections, Bible study, and spiritual growth have happened that lead them to believe God may be opening a door for a transition to a new ministry. At this point check their employment history for patterns and ask about why they felt God moving them along from those positions. Several short-term tenures are not always a problem (maybe they were in school, bi-vocational, leadership changes, or any number of reasons), but they can show if a candidate might have commitment issues or is unable to plant deep roots. I helped in the hiring process for a children's minister, and one candidate had a great resume until we got to his work history—every position was 12-18 months, he did seminary work at four schools but never graduated, and this led our team to decide this might not be a hire who would be a great long-term fit. Third, make it a priority to ask about when checking references.

Character and Hiring

Character is found in public and private qualities, both of which are rooted in integrity. When hiring someone, it is important to recognize that character is more important than competency when determining if someone is a good candidate to join your team. Character is the hardest to discern before spending extended time with a candidate. So how can a ministry team determine if a candidate has the character necessary to be a part of a healthy and effective team? It comes through personal assessment, references, and background checks.

The personal assessment is the opportunity for the candidate to speak honestly about their character, sharing with the lead pastor and ministry team victories and room for improvement with the private and public qualities listed in this chapter. Personal assessments shouldn't be an interrogation, but rather a conversation among people who are all striving towards Christlikeness.

References are crucial because they provide a look into the candidate's life from people who are close to them who can speak honestly to their character. I cannot emphasize how important references are for discerning the best candidate for your team, especially a reference who is willing to be honest about a candidate and not just give platitudes.

Finally, background checks provide an objective approach to discerning character. I would suggest doing a criminal background check, a credit check[lv], and a drug test. None of these are meant to imply a candidate has something to hide, but addresses issues that come up from ministering in a fallen world.

Competency and Hiring
When calling a potential ministry team member, you want to believe that the person you're calling is qualified and able to do the job. Many churches will ask for a sermon sample, which is a large part of a minister's skill set. Preaching is only one skill, however. Ask the candidate to share a sample of their work in their current church—something that would allow you to get a feel for how they do ministry such as a ministry manual or a summary of an outreach initiative. If the candidate maintains a blog or has some writing history, those provide a helpful assessment of the candidate's ability to communicate across different mediums, and will show what kind of thinker he or she is (strategic, visionary, or scrambled). The point is for the church to have a feel of the candidate's skill set, and every situation will be different. Have the candidate complete this ministry competency self-assessment to give you a feel for how they understand their own gifts, abilities, strengths, and weaknesses. Their self-assessment will helps determine on the front end whether or not a candidate would be a great match for the ministry team.

In addition to assessing a candidate's skill set, it's important to assess how that candidate's skills fit into the existing ministry team. For one, different candidates bring different sets of abilities, which allows for some fluidity in how the job description is written (discussed in the next chapter). It also allows the lead pastor to get a feel for the overall skill set of the ministry team, to see if a potential candidate can step in and fill a gap in what might be lacking, or if the candidate's skill set overlaps several others on the team already. Maybe your church is looking for a children's ministry leader, and a candidate comes along who has a high level of skill in pastoral care and writing. Instead of a cookie-cutter approach to hiring a children's ministry leader, you are now in position to strengthen your care ministry and your communication channels. You've now addressed three areas of ministry focus while still achieving the primary objective.

Chemistry and Hiring

A ministry team with healthy chemistry is a team that has the potential to be great instead of good. The ministry team that gets along, has great interpersonal rapport, and plays well together will create an environment where great things can happen. One without that kind of synergy will do good things, but may never reach their potential. Research from Harvard Business School reinforces the idea that chemistry matters.[lvi] Here are four ways to ascertain how a potential candidate might fit with and contribute to the chemistry on a team. Remember, a great candidate will add to team chemistry, while a bad candidate can destroy what might be a great team.

1) Do lunch or coffee and observe how he/she treats the servers. If a person is short, rude, or condescending to those taking their order or serving them, chances are that will happen in a ministry setting as well. On the other hand, if they're courteous, gracious, and generous (tips, not tracts), then that attitude will carry over to ministry interactions.

2) Invite the ministry team to give their gut reactions to the potential candidate. If you trust your team and think they are seeking out how to get better, their opinion carries a lot of weight. Hopefully there's a culture of transparency, honesty, and open communication among the team that would allow for even a potentially great candidate to be turned down because the existing team isn't sure they'd work well with him.

3) Check references. Call their references and ask good questions. This will give you as a hiring church great insight into how other ministry leaders see the candidate. If possible, see if the candidate would let you talk to a previous employer to ask how they were to work with—if they say no, don't sweat it.

4) Find out their personality. I think a lot of times bad chemistry is the result of personality clashes that can be avoided. So when bringing in a potential candidate, find out their personality using an assessment like DiSC. There are inexpensive options, and it's great to know how all the team members are wired so that the diversity of personality doesn't become a source of conflict.

Hiring a Lead Pastor

The process of hiring a lead pastor looks very different in most churches than the process of hiring associate staff. Many times a church's search for a lead pastor involves a separate committee approved by the congregation to seek out a candidate who is then presented to the church. Associate staff members may have a team who function to approve a candidate, but in many cases the existing leadership (especially the lead pastor) are the ones behind the hiring. This section is primarily geared towards lead pastors looking into moving to a new setting, though there will be some practical application for churches to consider.

First, the lead pastor has to be sure of his calling for the work of ministry. Can he clearly share his story of how God is at work in his life with the search team? Who along the way helped shape that calling? Can the candidate articulate why they might feel called to that local congregation? Did they send a resume or did someone refer them for the position—why? Have the candidate share with the search team why he feels like he is a viable candidate. The testimony of his calling is important for the church so they hear how the Spirit has called and equipped the candidate as an effective minister. It would be helpful to ask for a written testimony, which should provide clarity (and demonstrate his communication skills).

Second, the importance of character cannot be overlooked. As with hiring ministry team members, using personal assessment, references, and background checks provide a glimpse into the character of a potential lead pastor. In handling the self-assessment of the candidate, it would be helpful to ask about the candidate's "personal policies" when it comes to counseling, finances, balancing family and work, and protection from sexual immorality. Quickly discern whether or not you are dealing with someone who understands boundaries and is willing to put them in place. Avoid a candidate who is proverbially "playing with fire."

For references, ask for a pastoral colleague or denominational leader who might be able to speak into how the candidate was perceived by others outside the church. Was he known as someone who led well and was above reproach or was he someone who often left questions? For background checks, remember that a candidate may have lived in other states before, so it's important to make sure your checks include those states. Stories abound of pastors who cross state lines to avoid allegations of sexual abuse. For a candidate, honesty is always the best policy when dealing with a search team. Transparency about where God has brought him will show a search team that he is a credible and trustworthy person, even if they decide not to proceed with the hiring process.

Third, what skills does the candidate bring to the table? Look back through the list of personal, pastoral, and interpersonal skills listed in chapter four. Ask which are the candidate's strengths and weaknesses? What other skills does he have that could benefit the church? A background in finance, technology, or business management for example, has tremendous application in the church. Churches should seek to prioritize and list the skill set they would love to see in their next pastor.

Fourth, chemistry is hard to determine without being around the ministry team itself. You can get a sense, however, of how a candidate will fit within the church through the search team, who functions as a representative group of the congregation. A candidate should lean on the search team to learn the relational dynamics and needs of the congregation. At some point in the process, allow ministry team to spend time with the candidate. In those circumstances, make sure to focus on how the candidate "clicks" with the people he will spend most of his time with—pastors will spend more time with their staff than with the congregation. Learn how they fit together.

Reflection Questions

1. What policy and procedures do you have in place for hiring staff and leadership? Do they foster a team mindset?

2. Why is the recruiting/hiring phase so important for building a team?

3. How can you use recruiting/staffing groups to help build a team?

Chapter 7
Executing the Game Plan for a Ministry Team

By now, you should begin to see that it's possible to develop an effective ministry team through focus in four areas: calling, character, competency, and chemistry. As a ministry team centers on these, the possibility emerges for the staff to become a high-performing team that multiplies leadership and ministry effectiveness. It's important to keep the team's interests and ambitions as the overall team goal.[lvii] Remember, ministry teams don't answer to stakeholders, fans, or investors, they have a responsibility to Christ to lead the church well (Hebrews 13:7).

Developing a healthy ministry team involves knowing where the team is in the process. Gary McIntosh, a team leadership author, identifies four stages for teams: forming, norming, storming, and performing.[lviii] Forming is where relationships are built, trust is developed, and the lead pastor needs to take a more proactive approach.[lix] Norming is where a "team covenant" becomes the guiding principle of interaction, and the lead pastor becomes a supporter as the vision and values established by the team covenant guide the team. Storming is where leadership begins to face pushback. During this time, remember that "team members need a lot of emotional, spiritual, and personal support." In the storming phase, leadership can display empathy and endear themselves to the team or can appear aloof and distance themselves from the team. The performing phase is where the team as a whole is pursuing a collective course of action and the lead pastor has delegated significant authority and responsibility to team members. Growing as a team is difficult and requires the team members to be good team players, and the lead pastor to be active in the development of the team rather than removed from the team.[lx]

Here are four ways to apply the areas we have looked at through this book on developing an effective ministry team, from beginning to end. Each application carries with it a key word to guide the practice.

Hire Well (Key Word: Patience)
Hiring well means hiring the right *person*, not just filling a position. It's important to ensure that all four areas are incorporated into the hiring process (see chapter 6). Thom Rainer has observed that a church now spends anywhere from 9-18 months to search for a new pastor.[lxi]Search costs for a ministry leader could quickly run into thousands of dollars.[lxii] Doug Talley estimates a bad calling can potentially cost a church up to twice its annual budget.[lxiii] That is

why the key word for this application is *patience*. The right person cannot be rushed simply to fill a spot. It is always better to take a little longer to make sure the right team member is brought in than to rush the process to fill a spot or meet the immediate need. Churches need to prepare for hard questions and candidates should ask them. The candidate is willing to uproot his family and move his kids from their schools—so a church owes its candidates honest answers to hard questions.

It's hard to put a time frame on knowing when it's right to bring on a new hire in a church, because no two churches are the same with regard to expectation, culture, and health. Slower is better, but too slow can lead to stagnation. A rushed search process, however, can turn the entire search process into more of a beauty pageant than the calling of a pastor. I propose 5-8 months for a ministry team member, and 12-16 months for a lead pastor. These periods are subject to contextualization depending on any number of localized factors for each church. Slower is often better. But if a church is healthy, has solid leadership, a receptive congregation, and knows what they are looking for and even *who* they are looking for, they should not wait for the sake of waiting.

Evaluate (Key Word: Consistency)

In 2002, the Winter Olympics endured a figure skating scoring scandal. It ultimately led to a second gold medal being awarded, the suspension of a judge and a skating federation president, the arrest of a Russian mobster, and a complete overhaul of scoring in competitive figure skating. The scoring system in place at the time was inconsistent and manipulated for desired results. At issue was something even a high school student expects: that grading be done fairly. We should expect nothing else in ministry team evaluations, which is why the key word for this application is *consistency*. Consistent evaluations serve to reinforce the church's trust in its ministry team members, a catalyst for more effective and fruitful ministry, and constructive feedback on areas of improvement.

Timing of the evaluations should be done on a regular basis (Monthly, Quarterly, and Annually), which keeps the ministry team member aware of their progress, can help prevent significant leadership deficiencies and crises, and provide immediate affirmation. While the main and most formal evaluation is the annual one, which often determines compensation and annual goals, the value of informal monthly and quarterly evaluations cannot be overlooked. These serve as conversations to help a ministry team member towards accomplishing their goals and the team's goals, but can only happen if the team members interact with one another in a transparent and honest way.[lxiv] In these conversations, the personal/character element of pastoral leadership can be discussed—how the team member is leading his family, growing in his devotional life, pursuing purity, living with integrity, and working on Christlikeness.

A great format for the annual evaluation is the 360 format[lxv], involving a self-assessment, the supervisor, a peer on the ministry team, and from a leader who serves under the leadership of a team member. For example, the children's minister would be reviewed by himself, the lead pastor, the administrative pastor, and the elementary worship coordinator. LifeChurch.tv offers nine dimensions of leadership[lxvi], which shape their staff evaluations of open-ended questions for more reflection and input.[lxvii] Each church is different and should develop their own evaluation criteria, but the important thing is to have a plan for evaluating ministry team members. In the 360 format, multiple perspectives provide a complete picture of the team member, which, hopefully, the team member sees in the self-assessment.

Deploy & Redeploy (Key Word: Flexibility)

Rick Ankiel was a "can't miss" pitcher who had a promising career until he suddenly developed a case of the "Yips" and for no apparent reason was unable to throw strikes. After a few years in the minors, he re-emerged as a solid outfielder. His career was reignited by his ability to hit and throw accurately from the outfield. Other athletes have redefined themselves later in their careers to result in team success: R.A. Dickey became a knuckleballer, Michael Jordan developed a jumper, Charles Woodson moved to safety, and LeBron James became the Lakers functional point guard.

Deploy & Redeploy provides the opportunity for the ministry team to take full advantage of the gifts, skills, and callings that God has assembled, in order to accomplish the process of making disciples.[lxviii] It's the ability to play to the strengths of the team, to make additions to the team based on those strengths and areas of improvement, and to have existing team members transition into new roles based on need and ability. It's the constant pursuit of the dream team of ministry staff members who are competent, qualified, called, and complement each other. It's creating a climate where the health and effectiveness of the church is viewed as the most important thing, and the ministry team buys into a "whatever it takes" mindset that includes their job descriptions and shifting responsibilities.

Deploying is the easy part; it's the hiring process of a new team member. This was discussed in chapter 6 as we talked about assembling a ministry team. You look to fill a crucial strategic gap in your ministry team, so you hire the right person. They get a fresh job description (not a stock one or the last guy's), and the setup to succeed from day one with clear expectations, lines of accountability and authority, and the freedom to operate in their ministry area. Deploying is what many churches do well—bringing in team members who meet their needs and are able to hit the ground running. Sadly though, focusing only on deployment is short-sighted and doesn't factor in the changes to both the church and to the team members that come with time, experience, age, family circumstances or life changes.

Redeploying is more difficult, and requires a lot of flexibility. Redeployment requires a paradigm shift in how we view ministry job descriptions: *fluid* rather than *static*. Static views see the minister connected to the original job description, fitting the role he was hired for. A fluid view sees the ministry job description adjusting as the minister develops and matures, discovers additional areas of gifting, as team members transition out, or as the staffing needs change in the church. Fluid views of ministry job descriptions communicate the long-range value of a team member to the church, and recognize that ministry needs may change and require fresh thinking. Static views see the team member as fitting a role, and that the role is valued over the team member. Fluid views also cause lead pastors to develop strategic thinking and visionary planning. Static views don't, because the roles are predetermined and filled according to need. Fluid roles also create a climate of adjustment, flexibility, and newness among the ministry team and in the church. It keeps a ministry team and a church from falling into the quicksand of ineffective busyness, because volunteer and group structures respond to the fluidity of leadership and this keeps ideas and energy fresh among the ministry team and volunteers.

Leave Well (Key Word: Gracious)
Sadly, this is not something that is often handled well in churches. Our email boxes are filled with stories of ministers hurt by churches and churches hurt by ministers who left poorly. We need to change reality and handle ministry team members leaving better. The key word for this is gracious, which needs to be the description of both the ministry team member and the church, regardless of circumstances.

Graciousness happens by celebrating the successes and legacy of the ministry leader as he transitions out.[lxix] Even in a case of a youth minister being asked to step down, or a music minister who overspends his budget, many people were impacted by their leadership and ministry. Take an opportunity to thank the ministry leader for what he has done, bring in people who have been directly affected by his legacy, and take a love offering.

As I've talked to churches over the years, often there is a resentment towards the previous staff member, even a beloved staff member. The church feels like they were a stepping stone, the staff member left for greener pastures, or they feel insulted that a staff member would leave. Instead of this, a second way of leaving well is to view a staff member leaving as a commissioning opportunity rather than a loss. Take time to pray over the ministry leader and his family, write notes of encouragement, pray for their journey, and offer your excitement for their next assignment.

A third way to leave well is for both sides to speak well of one another after the departure. For the departing ministry leader, trashing your previous church tells the new church that you might throw them under the bus at the first sign of trouble, and compromises your trust and leadership cache in the new church. For the church to speak poorly of past leadership, it tells new leadership that it holds grudges, and won't be long before they do the same thing to new leadership. Both are unhealthy, and both parties need to do everything they can to live in peace with one another (Romans 12:18, Hebrews 12:14).

A fourth way to leave well is to build a culture of honesty and transparency on the ministry team. I read the story of a pastor who asked the elders to pray for him and his family because he was wondering if God had another assignment for him. They did and he recently announced his plans to transition out and plant a church with the full blessing and support of not only the elders, but the church. Sadly, I assume that such an approach is not normal for most ministry leaders. Something has to change. As I said in the Deploy & Redeploy application, ministry teams need to be flexible in how they view staffing and job descriptions. Sometimes leaders will leave. That is okay. Ministry leaders should be able to trust each other, and not hide the struggles of not being sure they are where God wants them.[lxx]

Final Thoughts
I hope that as you've read this book you've been challenged to see how important ministry teams are. More so, that you've seen that a team can be developed in your church. It's hard work, requires time, and may not see an immediate payoff, but it's a worthwhile pursuit. You will be far more effective as a church in reaching the community, discipling believers, engaging the lost, repairing broken families, and living on mission. Team building is more than simply coordinating programs, it's doing the work of

cultivating a healthy team through relationships and pursuing a common goal.

I want to leave you with a homework assignment. I want you to take some time this week to work on the team dynamics on your church staff. Don't do the awkward trust falls or go on some woodland retreat and do your best John the Baptist impression. Instead, go to lunch as a staff, play some pickup basketball, and set the example to be open with one another. Here are eight ways to develop an effective ministry team, no matter who you are on the organizational chart or what stage your ministry team is.

1. **Spend time together**: When we assume our staff is a team or we become so busy we never interact informally, we're missing out on the most obvious way to build a team: spending time together. Relationship capital is built this way and goes a long way toward building a healthy team. Time together does not need to be formal, focused on church business[lxxi], or spent with the entire team, but the lead pastor does need to be involved and engaged with the entire team.

2. **Champion others' ministries**: If you don't know what the other staff members are doing, you're not a team. Social media provides a great way to celebrate, promote, and endorse other ministries and team members. Lead pastors have the ability to champion from the platform, which encourages ministry team members and keeps the church aware of what the team is doing. Team members can involve themselves in areas outside their primary ministry area. As a youth minister, I try to be involved in children's events, which allows me to build relationships with the kids and their parents, but also to let the children's ministry team know I'm in their corner.

3. **Read together**: President Truman once said "all leaders are readers." If we're going to be serious about developing a healthy team and growing in ministry effectiveness, teams need to read together. It creates a conversation around the ideas and applications a book gives. Reading together needs to be challenging but accessible (read books that are easily grasped—sorry guys, now is not the time for the 1,000 page systematic theology), with a clear objective, and a rotation to keep the conversation going.[lxxii] Take time during staff meetings to discuss and apply the current reading.

4. **Have fun**: There's a time for laughter (Ecclesiastes 3), and there's a time for going bowling and watching everyone struggle to hit the pins. There need to be opportunities for the ministry team to enjoy one another's company. It shouldn't be forced;

nothing is more awkward than trying to have fun when everyone would rather have dental work. The fun together can serve as a bridge towards developing healthy relationships on the team. Some ideas include lunch for team members' birthdays, bowling, putt-putt, board game night, or karaoke.

5. **Get away**: It's so hard for a ministry staff to break the cycle of busyness to find time to get away from it all. Sunday always comes, there are counseling appointments, hospital visits to make, spreadsheets to balance, emails to answer, phone calls to make, and meetings to attend. In that cycle we often find ourselves in isolated busyness, where we work around people but not necessarily with them. Getting away breaks that routine, removes the distractions, and allows a team to focus. It doesn't have to be an overnight retreat; it can be an offsite afternoon. Getting away simply is breaking the routine and focusing on important things like team building or goals.

6. **Pray together**: When was the last time your ministry staff took time and really prayed for one another, with each other? So often ministry staffs pray for the sick list, needs of the church, and on the ministries of the church. Developing a ministry team involves praying for one another, creating the cord of three strands (Ecclesiastes 4:12). Build prayer networks among the team (groups of 3-4), who regularly pray for and with one another throughout the week, not just during meetings. Sadly, 37% of pastors are dissatisfied with their prayer lives,[lxxiii] and so many ministry leaders find themselves without a consistent or vibrant prayer life.[lxxiv]

7. **Dream together**: Mostly when we think of dreaming, we think of our sleeping dreams where we can fly, travel through time, or have the dog talk to us. But dreams play an active role while we're awake, they are where we can imagine what could be if we could be part of something truly special. On a ministry team, open up by asking questions like "what do you want our church to be like in 5-10 years?" Let the brainstorming and dreaming begin. It's the invitation for the team to get together and lay out ideas worth pursuing that lead to a healthier and more effective ministry. Without dreaming together, the weight of discouragement or cynicism can infect a ministry staff and keep it from achieving what God would desire.

8. **Serve together**: This provides a great way for the ministry team to serve in the community, whether it's at the local homeless shelter, painting at the retirement home, sorting cans at a food pantry, or something along those lines. It breaks up the normal routine and causes the team to function outside its comfort

zone. It also causes team members to see each other differently, and to recognize the humility needed for effective ministry. Finally, it tells the community that the church cares, and that the ministry team is invested in that community.

Lead pastor, you're coaching the team. Your role is to create a culture where the ministry team flourishes because everyone is on the same page striving for the same goals. You're using the four areas of calling, character, competency and chemistry to develop the team dynamic that leads to healthy and effective ministry. And you're aware of your role in actively promoting the team culture. If you're a ministry team member, your role is similar to a team captain. You're doing whatever it takes to see the ministry team succeed, you're backing your lead pastor as he works to develop a healthy team, and you're influencing the people you work with in your ministry area to join in on the common vision. This is important work, and you can do it. The church needs stronger, healthier, and more effective ministry teams, because the church is what Jesus left behind to see the world turned upside down.

Make it happen. Together Everyone Achieves More. Lead well. Serve well. See what Jesus can do with you and your ministry team when everyone is on the same team.

The results might surprise you, but that's what happens when we work for Jesus. Revelation 7:9 tells us that a multitude no one could number from every nation, language, and people will one day gather around Jesus to worship Him. Your ministry team can have a part in making that happen.

Now, get on the field and get to work!

Endnotes

[i]Frank LaFasto, and Carl Larson, *When Teams Work Best* (Thousand Oaks, CA: SAGE Publications, 25), 25.

[ii]George Cladis, *Leading The Team-Based Church* (San Francisco: Jossey-Bass, 1999), 100.

[iii]Stephen Macchia, *Becoming a Healthy Team* (Grand Rapids: Baker Books, 2005), 41.

[iv]Aubrey Malphurs, *Advanced Strategic Planning* (Grand Rapids: Baker Books, 2005), 222-23.

[v]LaFasto and Larson, *When Teams Work Best*, 3.

[vi]Bill Hybels, *Courageous Leadership* (Grand Rapids: Zondervan, 2002), 81.

[vii]J. Richard Hackman, *Leading Teams: Setting the Stage for Great Performances* (Boston: Harvard Business School, 2002), 41.

[viii]Ibid., 59.

[ix]Pat MacMillan, *The Performance Factor: Unlocking the Secrets of Teamwork* (Nashville: Broadman & Holman, 2001), 122.

[x]Patrick Lencioni, *The Five Dysfunctions of a Team* (San Francisco: Jossey-Bass, 2002), 189-90.

[xi]Macchia, *Becoming a Healthy Team*, 49.

[xii]Malphurs, *Advanced Strategic Planning*, 231.

[xiii]LaFasto and Larson, *When Teams Work*, xii.

[xiv]Cladis, *Leading the Team-Based Church*, xiii.

[xv]Rather than rely on an evaluation of a ministry leader or a ministry event based on "nickels and noses," the emphasis here is on "how well this reflected, promoted, supported, and

grew the ministry mission and vision of the church." But, as said in the chapter, without a clear direction for the ministry team, there really is no rudder guiding the ship and ministry team members will move back into the inertia of isolated busyness.

[xvi]Determining God's Call from CRU, http://www.cru.org/opportunities/careers/supported-staff/where-is-god-calling-you/gods-call.htm. Kevin DeYoung offers a great list at The Gospel Coalition: http://thegospelcoalition.org/blogs/kevindeyoung/2013/02/15/how-can-i-tell-if-im-called-to-pastoral-ministry/. Also, InterVarsity Christian Fellowship has a great list of questions to ask yourself here: http://www.intervarsity.org/blog/are-you-called-full-time-ministry.

[xvii]From "How Do You Know If You're Called to Pastoral Ministry?" at The ReSurgence, http://www.theresurgence.com/2014/02/04/how-do-you-know-if-you-re-called-to-pastoral-ministry.

[xviii]Charles Spurgeon, Lectures to My Students (Grand Rapids: Zondervan, 1954), 26.

[xix]If you've not seen this, look it up and YouTube.

[xx]http://en.wikipedia.org/wiki/50_home_run_club

[xxi]http://www.crosswalk.com/church/pastors-or-leadership/a-battle-for-integrity-11557444.html

[xxii]http://erlc.com/article/cultivate-integrity-in-ministry

[xxiii]Great books to help lead yourself or a ministry team through growing in spiritual disciplines include Don Whitney's Spiritual Disciplines for the Christian Life, Spiritual Disciplines for the Church, Richard Foster's Celebration of Discipline, and R. Kent Hughes' Disciplines of a Godly Man.

[xxiv]http://www.intothyword.org/apps/articles/?articleid=36562.

xxvStephen Covey has a great matrix on decision-making that looks at the Urgent and Important. For more, check out the *7 Habits of Highly Effective People*, or this website: http://www.usgs.gov/humancapital/documents/TimeManagementGrid.pdf.

xxviAs a note, remember not all debt is the same. If someone is younger and is carrying debt from student loans or educational expenses, that's different than someone who runs up high credit card debt buying lots of gadgets. In doing the credit check, also ask for an honest assessment from the candidate about their own understanding of their financial acumen.

xxviiMoney management programs like Dave Ramsey's *Total Money Makeover*, or *Crown Financial Ministry* provide ways for families to honor God with their finances.

xxviiiDaniel Montgomery of Sojourn Community Church in Louisville KY shared this on his blog about developing sermons with people in mind. It's worth passing along, even if it's not directly related to ministry teams. http://daniel-montgomery-sojourn.com/preaching-grid-how-do-we-preach-the-whole-counsel-of-god-to-everyone-2/.

xxixBob Newhart shows us a potentially flawed counseling technique in this video clip: https://www.youtube.com/watch?v=Ow0lr63y4Mw.

xxxFor a list of some helpful sites, Treasuring Christ offers those here: http://www.treasuring-christ.org/accountability-resources/.

xxxiRick Warren's 10 commandments are especially helpful here. http://pastors.com/maintaining-moral-purity-in-ministry/

xxxiiHere are some helpful sites on time management
Chuck Lawless offers 14 tips
http://thomrainer.com/2013/06/25/14-tips-for-time-management/
Time Management is Your Responsibility:
http://www.lifeway.com/churchleaders/2014/05/02/time-management-is-your-responsibility/

Joe Stengele offers 4 tips:
http://theresurgence.com/2014/02/27/4-time-management-tips-for-leaders
Boundaries for effective ministry: http://www.boundaries-for-effective-ministry.org/effective-time-management.html
Artie Davis: http://www.churchleaders.com/pastors/pastor-articles/156187-3-essentials-for-time-management.html

xxxiii http://www.accidentalcreative.com/productivity/use-time-chunks-to-eliminate-distraction/

xxxivBefore you email me your complaints, I get it that ministry is not always planned and is often filled with crises, emergencies, and unforeseen issues. In my opinion, some ministry leaders use those as excuses to not plan their life. If you've blocked time well, then you'll be able to make adjustments through the day/week/month to be able to maintain a healthy church/family balance. Sometimes your sermon prep will need to be adjusted because a husband found out his wife left him, or you can't meet your 3:30 counseling appointment because your daughter has the flu. Ministry happens. Like your schedule, but don't be married to it.

xxxvA great tool to determine this is the Eisenhower decision matrix, which can be found here:
http://www.artofmanliness.com/2013/10/23/eisenhower-decision-matrix/

xxxviHere's how I deal with this: Respond to text messages hourly, emails three times a day, and phone calls once a day. If you're a Covey person, you can arrange your day planner according to A-B-C priorities, or use a stoplight (Green = Low priority, Yellow = Medium, Red = Urgent). The 7 Habits can be found here: https://www.stephencovey.com/7habits/7habits-habit1.php

xxxviihttp://www.christianpost.com/news/pastors-and-time-44706/

xxxviiiDave Ramsey has some great tools on taking control of personal finances, including a free budgeting tool here:

http://www.daveramsey.com/tools/budget-forms/, and http://www.daveramsey.com/tools/budget-lite/.

xxxix LifeWay offers some help on church budgeting issues http://www.lifeway.com/lwc/files/lwcf_pdf_budget_basics_leaderlife.pdf

xlGary Bredfeldt, *Great Leaders, Great Teacher: Recovering a Biblical Vision for Leadership* (Chicago: Moody Publishers, 2006), 59.

xliFor some help on identifying these key people, check out a post I wrote on FAT people in ministry (Faithful, Available, and Teachable). I firmly believe that FAT people can do great things if they're given a little help along the way. You can find the post here: http://scottmdouglas.weebly.com/blog/building-a-volunteer-base-of-fat-people

xliiCrossings Ministries has a great thought on this called "The Beyond Effect" which is their process for teenagers to identify their burden and passion, and from that see what they can do to make an impact for Christ. I think the same thing applies to adults, as growth happens they find out what their gifts are and how they can make an impact in the church and Kingdom. You can find more on The Beyond Effect here: http://www.gocrossings.org/missions/the-beyond-effect/

xliiiYou can find a list of biblical counselors here: http://www.biblicalcounseling.com/counselors.

xlivhttp://www.peacemaker.net/site/c.aqKFLTOBlpH/b.5106139/k.B9F2/The_Gospel_of_Peace_Mirrored_Through_Peacemaking.htm

xlvhttp://www.buildingchurchleaders.com/articles/2005/090905.html

xlviKouzes & Posner identify five practices for leadership that can be learned and grown: Model the Way, Inspire a Shared Vision, Challenge the Process, Enable Others to Act, and Encourage the Heart. http://www.leadershipchallenge.com/about-section-our-approach.aspx

[xlvii]Bruce Katcher, "Does Team Chemistry Really Matter?" http://www.discoverysurveys.com/articles/itw-110.html

[xlviii]Jack McCluskey, "Farrell: Chemistry Crucial to Success" http://espn.go.com/boston/story/_/id/9399725/team-chemistry-culture-crucial-success

[xlix]http://www.torontosun.com/2011/05/10/liking-your-coworkers-could-help-you-live-longer-study.

[l]http://www.leadershipresources.org/blog/christian-ministry-burnout-prevention-signs-statistics-recovery.

[li]Christine Riordan, "We All Need Friends at Work" HBR, http://blogs.hbr.org/2013/07/we-all-need-friends-at-work/.

[lii]http://www.daveramsey.com/media/pdf/entreleadership_avoiding_enemies_of_team_unity.pdf. Those five are: poor communication, gossip, unresolved disagreements, lack of a shared purpose, and sanctioned incompetence.

[liii]http://www.psychologytoday.com/blog/trust-the-new-workplace-currency

[liv]http://hbr.org/2013/07/connect-then-lead/ar/1

[lv]A word here: if a candidate is a cash-only person who swears by the Dave Ramsey model, their credit score may not be very good. Always get context on a candidate ahead of time in case something pops up. Also, the criminal check may result in things showing up from long ago in their life. If the candidate is a person of integrity, they'll give you a heads up before running the check. If not, that might be a good red flag for your ministry team.

[lvi]http://blogs.hbr.org/2014/01/for-senior-leaders-fit-matters-more-than-skill/. What's really interesting about this idea is that skill alone can be overlooked if it leads to a better fit on the existing team. So for a church, how important must it be to make sure that not only does the candidate know what they're doing but that they'll fit with the ministry team? The benefit of resources like HBR is that they show us how people operate—

even men and women called by God are given to struggling with pride, organizational fit, and the learning curve of a new job. That's OK, it's a reminder of our constant need for grace.

[lvii]Aubrey Malphurs, *Advanced Strategic Planning* (Grand Rapids: Baker Books, 2005), 232. Malphurs doesn't intend for the lead pastor to not have a vision for the church, and to lead the ministry team in that direction. Rather, he points the ministry team towards the principle of Philippians 2:4 where Paul urges Christians to look after the interests of others. The synergy on a team of seeking the best for the whole should lead the team to make decisions that better the team, and as a result of that the best for the church.

[lviii]Gary McIntosh, *Staff Your Church for Growth: Building Team Ministry in the 21st Century* (Grand Rapids: Baker Books, 2000), 179-82.

[lix]For more on the stages of leadership and involvement towards followers, check out Situational Leadership II from Ken Blanchard.

[lx]McIntosh uses the analogy of a van to describe the ministry team. Everyone is on the van and can contribute their opinion of where the van is going, the directions, where to eat, etc. But at the end of the day, only one person is driving the van—the lead pastor. Others can take the wheel as situations arise, but in reality there can only be one principal driver.

[lxi]http://thomrainer.com/2014/09/22/six-updates-churches-pastoral-vacancies/.

[lxii]The Simpson Baptist Association in Mississippi gives a list of prospective pastor expenses in the search process here: http://simpsonbaptist.com/PastorSearchpt2.

[lxiii]https://chogministryconnector.com/downloads/pdfs/Senior%20Pastor%20Search%20Process%20Tips.pdf

[lxiv]Tony Morgan says this, especially to senior pastors: "Because of this, the senior pastor needs to fight against becoming an isolated leader. As your church grows, you can't isolate yourself from your team by staying in the safe confines

of your office or your green room. You need to engage with your key leaders. They need to see you and hear from you often. If you don't engage the team, the team will not engage with each other."
http://tonymorganlive.com/2014/04/23/ministry-silos-leadership/#sthash.GFtLUL7k.dpuf

[lxv]For the lead/senior pastor, the supervisor may be a personnel oversight team, or a party mutually designated party (trustworthy deacon, pastor of another church in the community, or another ministry team leader). Again, this is dependent on the polity structure and church culture.

[lxvi]The 9 dimensions are Mission, Team, Interpersonal, Trustworthiness, Drive for results, Collaboration/Teamwork, Team leadership, Communication skills, and Personal development.

[lxvii]For example, rather than asking "Did Jim have an effective year serving as music minister?" the question should be phrased "Give some specific examples of Jim's effectiveness as our music minister this past year."

[lxviii]Aubrey Malphurs, *Advanced Strategic Planning* (Grand Rapids: Baker Books, 2005), 226.

[lxix]I feel I should put a slight disclaimer here: moral failure. If in the event a ministry leader has to be removed because of a moral failure (affair, theft, pornography, addiction, etc.), public recognition and celebration should be tempered. In this event, the emphasis of the church needs to turn to the spiritual health and support for the minister and his family. Many churches throw out their fallen ministry leaders, rather than provide them the counseling, support, and love they need. The Kingdom is much larger than a particular local church, and a fallen minister has ripple effects that extend far beyond one local congregation. See the discipline, healing, and hopefully the restoration of a fallen minister as the opportunity to build the Kingdom and protect the overall reputation of the gospel, not the chance to pile on to a devastated family.
[lxx]I did a survey of almost 500 associate pastors and many of them weren't sure if they were where God wanted them, and many did not feel they could share with their lead pastor their

desire for a new field of ministry service. Only a few reported that they had a healthy enough relationship with their pastor to open up about their long-range career goals.

[lxxi]I found this during my doctoral thesis, that on high performing ministry teams that were seeing younger leaders discipled and raised up to more visible and influential leadership positions, there was an informal but intentional relational dynamic on the ministry team. On those teams, the lead pastor maintained an open door policy and made himself available to his ministry staff. Also, the associate pastors on those teams made a commitment to engage one another and their lead pastor often by bridging the differences between personal and professional relationships. They demonstrated a genuine care for and friendship with one another.

[lxxii]The rotation I propose is: devotionals, ministry-focused books, spiritual growth, biography, and books on leadership. Every ministry context is different, but should try to read from a wide variety of fields and sources.

[lxxiii]http://www.churchleaders.com/pastors/pastor-articles/150915-us-statistics-on-prayer.html.

[lxxiv]http://betweenthetimes.com/index.php/2013/10/21/equipping-pastors-part-8-the-pastor-and-his-prayer-life/.

Made in United States
Troutdale, OR
02/22/2024

17871398R00051